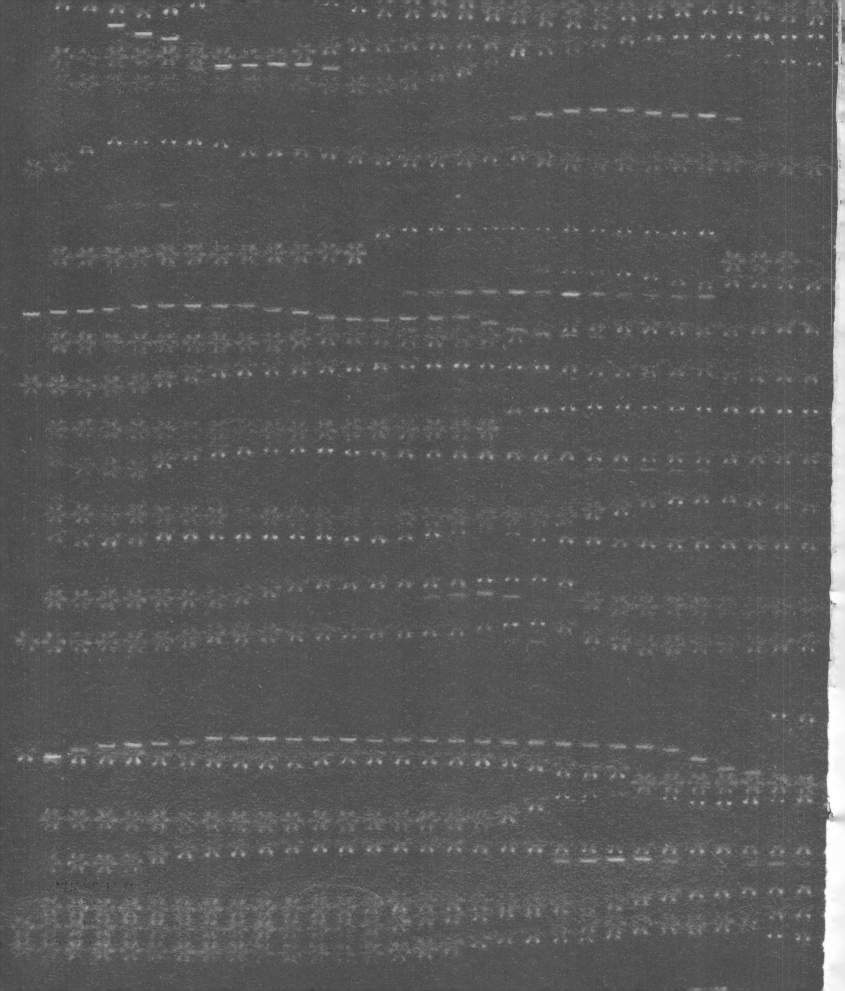

Kelly
Slater

For
the
love

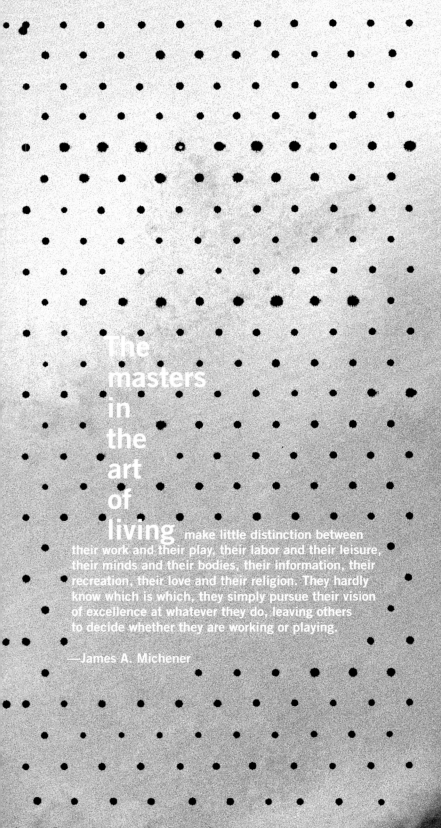

The masters in the art of living make little distinction between their work and their play, their labor and their leisure, their minds and their bodies, their information, their recreation, their love and their religion. They hardly know which is which, they simply pursue their vision of excellence at whatever they do, leaving others to decide whether they are working or playing.

—James A. Michener

Kelly
Slater

For
by
Kelly
Slater
with
Phil
Jarratt
the
love
Foreword
by
Jack
Johnson

Page 192 constitutes a continuation of the
copyright page.

Library of Congress Cataloging-in-Publication Data
available.

ISBN: 978-0-8118-6222-6

Manufactured in China

Designed by Martin Venezky's Appetite Engineers

10 9 8 7 6 5 4 3 2

Chronicle Books LLC
680 Second Street
San Francisco, California 94107
www.chroniclebooks.com

**Phil
Jarratt
would
like
to
thank:** PT for a good idea, Paul and Kiku for the
Center St studio, the Bradburns for the spare room
in Bidart, Bob McKnight for just saying yes, Tim
Richardson at Quiksilver, Jeff Hall at A-Frame and
Jeff Divine at Surfers Journal for the hard yards on
the pix, Harry Hodge and Bruce Raymond for ongoing support, Belly Slater for making me laugh,
David Rensin for wise counsel, Terry, Noah and the
crew at Sonar, Jack Johnson, Shelby Meade, KS, of
course, Peff Eick for the loan of the perfect old guy
Cloudbreak board, Sarah, Matt, Jake and the crew at
Chronicle for their patience and professionalism, and
Jackie for just about everything else.

pages 1, 2–3:
At
work
and play,
Cloudbreak, '05.

this spread:
Western
Australia, '07.

In late 2006, I was traveling with my friend Bruce Gilbert and had just won my eighth

world title. We'd spent the past two years and more traveling to all corners of the globe together (why are they called corners?) and he'd taken photos of pretty much all of it, so we thought we'd compile a scrapbook of our adventures.

We decided to start by putting together shots he'd taken in that time, collect others from friends and photographers we know that filled in the gaps, and go from there to build a story of one amazing period of time in both our lives. Our idea was just to make a scrapbook, really. But as we went on, the idea transformed into something a little different.

As I write this I'm in California after having surfed and won the first two events of the 2008 World Tour in Australia—the Quiksilver Pro at Snapper Rocks, run by my sponsor of eighteen years, and the Rip Curl Pro at Bells Beach. I have been in the mind-set that I won't complete a full year on the tour, again sort of going into semiretirement, which I did for three years after winning my sixth title in 1998 and being completely burned out on living the competitive life.

I finished third in the world last year and found at the end of it (and actually during it) that I wasn't nearly as enthusiastic about competing at the one thing that has always been my first love. I've always said that if I wasn't loving what I was doing, I would simply do something else. Being in this place, having two wins under my belt, feels good for sure, but at the same time I'm still not certain it's exactly what I want to be doing at this point in my life. I'll keep going for however long feels right, and I'm sure the right thing will happen. And it's pretty cool to be a few years past what many people thought was my prime and still be having some wins. Kinda hard to just walk away from it when that's happening!

I think we surfers are mostly addicts of some sort or another, using waves as our fix. I've probably spent most of the years of my life using surfing as my getaway from things I didn't want to think, feel, or deal with on some level. Many times surfing was the only thing I wanted to feel at all. Yet at the same time, I've been intrigued by questions of life, death, family, music, politics, spirituality, and many other things. For me surfing is my own way to read the world, or at least it's the place from which I can read things most easily.

When I started out on the world tour, I was really excited by the idea of it but basically bored by the standard of surfing. That's a strong statement, but I actually saw very clearly how easy it could be at that time to win a world title against what was being done by the top guys. I don't say that with any spite or disrespect for the surfers who came before me at all. If not for guys like Martin Potter, Tom Carroll, Tom Curren, Occy, and many more heroes of mine before them, I wouldn't be anywhere close to the level I'm at, nor would I have a love like I do for surfing. They planted all the seeds I grew from.

As a grommet, and even as a young pro surfer, nothing else mattered like riding waves. (Well, once in a while there were other things, but I found girls way more complicated than waves!) But as we grow and experience things our minds grow, our questioning grows, our ideas get bigger and broader, and the purpose of our lives becomes clearer. Life and love is far more important, I know, and surfing is just one aspect of my or anybody's life.

One of my favorite days ever, Soup Bowls, Barbados.

My life's a collection of so many people, places, thoughts, experiences, and random connections that together create such a vast web of excitement, adrenaline, adventure, and sometimes confusion, which I'm sure very few people get to experience in their whole lives, let alone every day. I do have a few obligations here and there to actually work, but for the most part I'm about the luckiest guy you'd ever meet. I literally get paid to go surfing every day. When the waves are good and I have somewhere to be, you can pretty much rest assured that I'm one of the only people who can get away with just telling the truth—that I was out surfing and the waves were good and I just couldn't make it on time or at all. And while I'm out in the water, I'll probably meet some chiropractor or musician or sushi chef who'll invite me to come by and get fixed up, play some music, or have a meal. Dream job, and life, as far as I'm concerned.

So why am I making this book? To be honest with you, as it has evolved I've spent time asking myself that same question. I'm actually at odds with it on some level. Making a book about yourself seems like a pretty narcissistic, self-centered thing to do. Also, once you write something, it's in print and there's not a lot you can do about it. In some way this book kind of made itself. Many people are involved in this process. One of my greatest passions in life is connecting people, and since I'm in touch with so many people around the world, this might be a good way to bring all that together. A few years back, I wrote another book (with Jason Borte) called *Pipe Dreams* that was basically an autobiography. I had the same doubts about that one, but I can't tell you how many people have come up to me since and told me they read it and it helped them in some way to look at their own life. To be honest, I've only read it once—while I was doing the final edit of the book. It was confronting for me. I was sure I'd upset my family and maybe some friends, but I also hoped it would open up some things in a positive if indirect way for us, and that happened. With this book I've tried, for the most part, to let the pictures tell the story, or at least direct where it goes. I've also questioned how far to go in expressing my own beliefs and thoughts about things.

Last year, Bruce (Gilbert) showed me some antiwar art that I put on my boards. After competing on that board, I was asked on Surfline to give an explanation of the art. I got angry mail about it from a number of people, some of which was sent my way to read. I know that even some of the people at Channel Islands, who make my boards, were confused by the statement. I was floored by some of the things people had to say, but I guess so were they by my opinions. The antiwar stance can be a strangely hated one. In a nutshell, I think we were crazy as a nation to have gone to Iraq, and for that matter, Afghanistan. I was telling friends at the time how we were being lied to about the reasons for war, and most of that has come out since. This airbrush I had on my boards was my silent but visible way of saying this. Coincidentally, I rode that board for the only time in competition last year in Chile—a democratic country that thirty-five or so years ago the United States covertly helped to overthrow. Riding it was not planned and I was, in fact, going to skip that event, but looking back now it seems fitting that I got to ride that board in Chile. Not that it's some grand statement in the big scheme of things, but in my own small way I was able to visibly state my opinion through it.

For the Love covers a few of these topics, and I'm sure more than a few people will question why a surfer is even talking about them. I guess you can always put the book down!

I have friends in all walks of life. I've learned something from each of them in their own way and answered many questions for myself by just listening and talking to people all over. My life is very public in some ways and very private in others. I'm in a strange place because I believe that we create absolutely everything that occurs in our lives from which to learn something, and so I sometimes wonder how I ever found myself in some of the situations I've been in. I've had a few tough lessons along the way, so if nothing else, I've got life experience.

When I was a kid, I wanted not necessarily to be famous but to achieve the things I set out to do, but there were many things that molded me into who and what I am today. I'd like to think it's all positive and good, but we're all also directed by bad experiences. When I was a kid, I had experiences that were embarrassing, heartbreaking, funny, sad, and so on, just like anyone else. Like when I was in love with this girl who always liked the older, more popular guys. Then I'd end up seeing her making out with "that guy" at a party. The only time she really seemed to take much notice of me, from my perspective, was when she saw me in a surf magazine. Or when I got beat in an arm-wrestling match at school by a girl in front of all my friends when I was about fourteen years old! Or how winning a pro-am contest that same year against all the local pros might've locked me into a certain direction in life that I was set to go in. I also wonder what things were like for my older brother, Sean, when I was really starting to do well and get photos in surf mags all the time and video sections in the new surf movies when at some point he wasn't and what effect that had on him. Or how it feels for people to always ask him what I'm up to, seemingly unconcerned about what's happening for him. (It's become a joke between us.) Or for Stephen, my younger brother, who basically grew up without us, as we traveled so much. And for my mom who raised three boys on her own without much money and not a lot of help from anyone else (although now it seems like everyone we know changed our diapers and babysat for us at some point when we were kids, right?). Sometimes when I'm remembering where I've been and picturing where I'm going, I think about how experiences like those might've molded me and patterned me as I grew up to deal with life the way I do. Sometimes I look back at everything and imagine if some things could have been different or whether they were all aligned in this perfectly organized fashion to create a desired outcome, not like predestiny but more of a connecting-the-dots-and-things-keep-making-sense kind of thing, going on the feeling in your gut. Life is dynamic, and winning and loss are parts of the equation. I find that I've learned most when things have seemed to go horribly wrong, and in the end they end up just the way you would want it.

Kalani and I.

This book was first called *A Thousand Words* due to the fact that the pictures tell the story and guided the things I chose to talk about. We changed the title to *For the Love* for a number of reasons. Originally, *For the Love* was an idea we had for a surf film showing all the things I love about surfing and my life. The film never got made, but this book is an extension of that and basically talks about many things I am interested in and have passion for in life. Ironically enough, *For the Love* was also an ongoing theme that friends of mine had during interviews with Phil Jarratt. They basically all said they wanted me to find true love and happiness.

First off, thank you, guys— everyone who made this book possible and the words that many people will see through your eyes as well as the photos supplied by all the photogs and friends from around the world. This is basically a compilation of photos throughout my whole career that tell "a thousand words." I've (unintentionally) left out a lot of important people in my life for many different reasons. Well, probably there just wasn't a photo to tell that story right now. I'll have to search out some more shots and talk about those one day if I do another of these. And to my friends who were worried about me finding love, I'm pretty sure I've found it. Thanks for reading.

Luke Munro, me, and Kelly on the Quiksilver Crossing at Europa, 2002. We all look pretty happy in this photo but a few days later Luke was not smiling. He was being pulled into the back of the customs hall at the airport. Kelly had stuck a fish in his board bag as a going away present, and Luke had some explaining to do. We were on our way home from a surfless surf trip. Kelly was staying on to wait for waves. He wasn't in a hurry to leave. He never really is. JJ

I think I was about twelve when I first encountered Kelly Slater.

In those days we used to surf the beach breaks at Ehukai a lot and we'd come in and eat a bowl of cereal on the front porch of our house and watch the other guys surf. I remember seeing Kelly riding a mango-colored board and he did this really long floater, the longest floater I'd seen anybody do. I remember all of us on the porch staring in disbelief. It was one of the craziest maneuvers we'd ever seen.

It wasn't long after that floater that we met. He was three years older than me, which doesn't mean anything now, but when you're a teenage kid it's different. I looked up to him rather than meeting as equals but the age gap changed as we became good friends. He became part of our group, we hung out, surfed, later we both learned to play guitar.

I've never known anyone who loves to surf more than Kelly. Any conditions, any board, he just loves riding waves. I think he could go on and win as many world titles as he wants to.

If I had to describe Kelly to someone I'd start out by saying he's usually about an hour late. If you don't know him you'd think he was being rude, but if you do know him, you would know his lateness is caused by respect for the person he's talking to, not disrespect for the person who is waiting. Whether it's surfboard design or some oil company conspiracy theory, he gets right into the conversation and he's not leaving until it's finished. And he's a great listener.

He's limber, freakishly loose. I remember on a surf trip, waking up one morning and coming out to the living room and he's stretching with his feet behind his ears! I remember thinking, how can he do that? So he's limber, he's late, and he listens. That's my take on Kelly.

For the future, I just hope that he's happy, because when your job is winning world titles, that's a hard thing to come down off of. But I think he'll be able to move on to the next phase and grow old gracefully.

11

WAITING FOR KELLY

This book could have been called *Waiting for Kelly.*

Several of his friends suggested it. This was certainly my experience more often than not over the many months of interviews and brainstorming that went into the making of this book.

Constantly in demand, Kelly retreats into Kellyworld, where nothing is more important than the present moment. In Kellyworld, as former champion Shaun Tomson once noted about being inside the barrel, time stands still. There are no schedules, no deadlines.

It's difficult to fault that logic, and the many people who love Kelly Slater simply don't. If you're sitting somewhere between love and a paycheck, however, sometimes it's funny, sometimes it's infuriating. Consider the following log of text messages between Kelly and me on the morning of September 5, 2007, when I was supposed to be meeting him in Newport Beach, California:

KS 3:11 A.M.: Phil, stayed in LA so just text me before heading south. If I'm not up and down there we'll meet up here. Kelly.

PJ 6:55 A.M.: Hi Kel, let me know the plan. Ready to go when u r. Phil.

PJ 8:26 A.M.: Yo! You up yet? I'm hot to trot!

KS 9:37 A.M.: Just opened my eyes. Still in bed asleep. Let me think of a plan. Where are you?

PJ 9:39 A.M.: PCH South coming into Santa Monica.

KS 9:53 A.M.: There's a spot at 26th and San Vicente that's pretty good to eat. We can meet there. I think it's go left on San V and right to 26.

PJ 9:55 A.M.: On my way.

KS 10:01 A.M.: Brentwood Country Mart is the place. Just jumping up now. Was awake to 5am on my computer, hate those things.

PJ 10:34 A.M.: KS, I'm here!

KS 11:01 A.M.: I'm trying to come but been stuck for 20 mins with construction in dead end street. Could be another 10.

PJ 11:03 A.M.: Can't you get out and walk! Don't sweat it, I'll order another bucket of coffee.

It was a silly closer. Kelly Slater wasn't going to be sweating this, although the fact that he'd even kept me informed of the morning's small disasters was an unusual concession to the normal human rules of engagement. And when he finally arrived, we sat in the midst of lunching moms and their screaming kids for four or five hours while he talked into a recorder, ruminating on life and love, riffing on surfing, music, and golf. For a while we were both inside the bubble that is Kellyworld, and that night he sent me a text containing a quotation from James A. Michener he thought appropriate, and a heartfelt thank-you for a good day's work. I was touched despite myself.

Another day on 'The Crossing.'

13

This is the enigma that is Kelly Slater, the greatest surfer ever. (Anyone who tells you he isn't simply hasn't been paying attention these past fifteen years.) Kelly has rewritten the record books, transcended his sport and his culture to become a truly famous person, not to mention a scratch golfer and a handy singer/songwriter. He has acted, too, but let's not go there. His love life has involved a string of glamorous, famous women, and the price he has paid for that is to become tabloid fodder, a paparazzi target. He is mobbed at the beach, and kids line around the block to get an autograph at store appearances. Everyone wants a piece of Kelly, and I include myself: who are we, those of us who lunge at him with our cameras, recorders, posters to sign, and causes to bless, to deny him the sanctuary of Kellyworld?

It's easy to see why everyone is attracted to him. If ever a person was in the right place when the blessings were showered down. . . . His incredible, beautiful, brilliant, and fearless surfing defines him, but beyond that he is an extraordinary, intelligent, articulate, and resourceful individual, one who is wise in many ways, loving and kind in many others, and—this is not easy for a crusty old surf-writer—beautiful to behold. He can also be a pain in the butt, self-absorbed, conceited, and dare I say it, flaky.

However, as many of his friends told me in the course of preparing this book, he is a person whose presence in your life makes you feel special. He is not an easy friend to make, but when you have his trust, you have it forever. Sometimes the great and the good look just like the rest of us. Sometimes they radiate a magnetic energy. Kelly glows. One friend said, "When Kelly is introduced to people who don't know who he is, they realize immediately that he is special, a superachiever. He projects that aura."

This is Kelly's second book. The first, *Pipe Dreams*, ghostwritten by Jason Borte, is Slater's autobiography; it tells the story of a kid from a broken home in central Florida who, like so many great athletes, used his physical gifts to both shield him from hurt and deliver him from a life of ordinariness and struggle. Kelly and Borte, a former pro surfer himself, tell the story in a compelling way, but they did not answer all our questions about how Kelly became who he is and how he does what he does. How could they? Kelly's life is a work in progress. Since then, his competitive comeback has added two more world surfing titles to his credit, and his life continues to unfold.

Just thirty-five years old in 2007, the year in which *For the Love* was compiled, most of Kelly Slater's life still lies ahead of him. Yet this year marked the beginning of the end of the competitive chapter in his life, even as he roared from behind in a late—and ultimately unsuccessful—charge toward a ninth world surfing title. Kelly wanted to mark the end of his first ridiculously successful career with a portrait in words and pictures of the person he really is. It is a portrait that will surprise many people because the straitjacket of fame reduces most public utterances to the shallowness of the thirty-second sound byte. A deep and diverse thinker, Kelly is equally comfortable with hydrodynamics and metaphysics, with Teahupoo and Chomsky.

I had known Kelly for about ten years when this book was suggested to me by my friend Peter Townend, who in 1976 became the first world professional surfing champion. The concept was to get inside Slater's head and surround his thoughts with amazing photos, and this is pretty much what we have ended up with. But there was one problem. I wasn't part of Kellyworld, didn't even have visiting rights. In fact it seemed that for most of our encounters in different parts of the world, in my capacity as a Quiksilver marketing manager, I was a Them and not an Us. If I wasn't thumping on his Munich hotel room door to drag him off to a press conference, just as one of his many romances came to a teary, tragic, and traumatic end, I was breaking into his Snapper Rocks apartment to deliver five hundred sheets of paper that had to be autographed by tomorrow. Kelly doesn't necessarily hate people who try to make him do stuff, when there's a crisis in Kellyworld, but he can certainly make you feel uncomfortable.

So it was with some trepidation that I approached our first book meeting in Los Angeles early in 2007. I figured I'd lay it on the table, then get out of the way and let someone with better rapport do the legwork. But Kelly signaled early that he wanted to work with me, and even better, he had strong views on what he wanted to say and how it should be presented. We started work immediately and continued as he flew from one side of the world to the other on what began to look like his swan song on the pro tour.

I can't say it's been easy. Too often the drawbridge would go up, and I'd find myself on the wrong side of the moat that protects Kellyworld. But I also sometimes became privy to Kelly's close-knit circle. Some of his friends became my friends, and through them I learned as much about Kelly as I learned from my conversations with the man himself. But in the end, it is Kelly's singular voice and worldview that enlightens this book. I merely let myself into Kellyworld from time to time, straightened the furniture, and pulled back the curtains to let the world in . . . just a little.

Finally, a confession. I was a Kelly fan going into this book and I'm a bigger Kelly fan coming out. I hope you feel the same way.

As we went to press with the second edition of For The Love, Kelly achieved numerically the world title he seemed to have achieved psychologically months before. Although statistically it was not the biggest margin in World Championship Tour history—it wasn't even Kelly's own biggest margin—it was the most decisive world title campaign ever. Kelly's confidence never wavered from the moment he took the first event by the scruff of the neck, and then backed it up with a freakish win at Bells. His few faltering steps along the way were shrugged off and immediately replaced with a new surge of precision surfing, for which his closest rivals had no answer. We still don't know if this is the end of the beginning or the beginning of the end. All we can do is enjoy the ride with the greatest surfing champion ever.
PJ

This was on a Young Guns 2 trip. We were on this huge boat with a helicopter (which was embarrassing when other surfers were around and we busted that thing out!) and Jet Skis, and pretty much everything you could ever want on a surf trip. The boat made a huge wake, more like a hill than a wave. You can't tell here, but it's about head-high at the top of that mound of water. At one point we had five guys riding it at once, but it was a bit dangerous because you can run into the back of the boat. It's funny how that cloud is sitting above my head like a halo.

1

For the fun

How it all began.

This
was
on
the
same
Young
Guns
trip as
the
previous
pages.
This day
was insane
at a right
that I'd
been hearing
about from
friends for
a few years.
During the
morning there'd
been 25 to 30
guys out but as
the tide dropped
everyone took a
break. Only about
5 of us stayed
out and there were
two to three barrels
on most waves.
I was totally
embarrassed
when we busted
out the helicopter
and it was so loud
and in your face
for everyone, but it
really gave a great
perspective on the
wave. "You can clearly
see how shallow this
wave is. Not a good
place to fall. One of
my most memorable
sessions."

Probably my earliest memory is being about three years old

and visiting my best friend's grandfather's house down the street. Grandpa was known as "Peepaw" and his wife was "Meemaw." Peepaw did yardwork all day and whistled. He was an amazing whistler. I was drawn to it like the Pied Piper. I'd wander up the street, often without my friend, and sit in Peepaw's sandbox and listen. My mom would find me there, running the sand through my fingers, wide-eyed and listening to Peepaw's melodies, and watching him tend to his garden.

I guess Peepaw was my first hero. He took us for rides in his boat, caught trout almost every morning, taught us how to ride bikes. One time when I was about five I ran into his sprinkler in the yard and got metal stuck in my knee. Peepaw busted out his knife and just cut it right out. No tetanus shot, no one got sued, no hospital . . . they were the good old days.

Because it's the South and it's small-town, I guess people expect Cocoa Beach to be redneck. If you went a ways inland from our town, I don't doubt it was, but because of its proximity to Cape Canaveral, the "Space Coast" was cushioned from much of that. My town was reasonably affluent, middle class—and almost totally white. People didn't get worked up about the big issues in Cocoa Beach.

I wasn't raised with any strong religious beliefs or political views, although if you'd asked me, I would have said I was a Republican because that's what my parents said they were. Dad was a pretty simple kind of a guy who never got too heated about things, and he took a lenient view of the stuff that my brothers and I got up to. Mom had a more black-and-white view of things. Although she wasn't a disciplinarian by any stretch of the imagination, she was stricter than Dad. I couldn't cuss or get in fights when Mom was around.

When I look back now, I see two distinct phases of my childhood. The first ended when I was about eight. Up to that point I was kind of a class bully, always getting into fights and on the verge of big trouble at school. It's hard to believe when you look at the earliest photos of me surfing, but I was a bit pudgy and bigger than most of the kids in class. Up to second grade, no one wanted to mess with Kelly Bobby! I fought with one kid, Owen, almost every day, and we'd both have to sit against the wall all through recess. There was always a class debate about which of us was the tougher, and if someone said Owen was, I'd probably have to fight them over it.

Right around this time my parents started to fight horribly, and my mom tried to kick my dad out of the house. Something inside me clicked. I didn't want to be a fighter anymore. I changed from being aggressive to almost submissive overnight. Part of it was not wanting to stress Mom out any more than she was. I became quite introverted, and despite the fact that people see me performing in public and think I'm outgoing, I still am.

I started messing around with surfing from about the age of five,

but it was just a summer thing. Both my parents encouraged it but never pushed it. My dad surfed quite a bit, but not very well. It was something he enjoyed. After school I'd generally go straight to the beach and surf if there were any kind of waves at all, but if it was flat, I was never concerned because I had so many other interests throughout my childhood—tennis, football, basketball, fishing, wakeboarding, and I was really into ping-pong—but surfing always seemed to overshadow them.

I realized that surfing might become more than a recreation when I was twelve and I won a contest. The prize was a trip to Hawaii. My first picture in a magazine came when I was ten, and I made the local paper that year, too. At twelve I had a black-and-white photo over a third of a page in *Surfing* magazine. I was away! My first national cover came when I was fifteen and *Surfing* ran an air maneuver at Sebastian Inlet. Oakley had stickers in separate letters at the time, so I'd grabbed a couple of them and shuffled the letters to spell my name, and had "KELLY" stickered across the front of my board.

My first surf shot taken by my Dad in knee-deep water.

I wanted to be sponsored from the very beginning. When I got one of my first boards, I wanted them to put a "TEAM" sticker on it, so I could be on the local Salick Brothers surf team. The Salicks thought long and hard about putting me on the team (or maybe they just waited a while to be nice) but finally decided against it. My parents kept paying retail for my boards. I was more fortunate than a lot of kids because I never had to work jobs after school, so I could focus on my surfing. When I was fourteen a friend was making some money doing yardwork for people around town, so I started picking weeds with him one day. We got totally engrossed in picking the smallest weeds, and after two hours the lady fired us both. That was the only real job I ever had, and I think I made ten bucks. Later, when my brother Sean and I were sponsored by the Sundek brand, they couldn't pay us because we were amateurs, so they tried to give us a job stacking clothes, but that only lasted one day and they ended up just giving us the money under the table.

Young Guns
Trip, 2005.

My first surfing hero was "Buttons" [Kaluhiokalani].

I saw him in a movie with Larry Bertleman when I was about eight. The whole world seemed crazy about Bertleman at the time, but it was Buttons who caught my eye. Buttons was forever goofing around on a wave, having fun, switching stance in the middle of a turn, big smile on his face. He seemed to push the boundaries every time he took off, and I loved his attitude.

One day we were down at the beach when someone arrived with the latest surf mag. On the cover was this wild-looking guy doing an air so high you couldn't really see the wave below it. He wasn't that much older than us, and it was so exciting to see someone so young doing something so completely different. This was Martin "Pottz" Potter, and he was my new hero.

Of course, we knew a little about aerial surfing. We'd seen photos of Davey Smith on the West Coast doing them. Locally, a guy named John Holman had been throwing frontside air 360s virtually at will since the late '70s, while my friend and mentor Matt Kechele had pioneered the "Kech air," and Pat Mulhern and John Futch were always trying airs. I'd played my part, too. As a really little kid I'd gone through a phase where all I wanted to do was kick out of the wave and fly as high into the air as I could. I didn't grab my board, just went off into space. I called this highly functional maneuver my "Superman," but it definitely wasn't the superman you see today.

This was something else. I looked at Pottz and saw the future of surfing, but he, too, had to justify the functionality of his maneuvers. It took him a while to do that and to win a world championship. The thing about Pottz was you could never count on him to make the wave. He always looked about to fall, but you knew if he stayed on his board, he was going to win by a mile. I thought his approach was just so much better, but it's hard to win if you can't stay on.

23

Focusing at
the OP East,
Sebastian
Inlet, FL,
1989.

Watching Pottz so intently while my surfing was just starting to develop taught me a valuable lesson. He was so reckless it seemed like he didn't care, and I couldn't understand that. There is more method than madness in competing, and sometimes you have to rein in your impulse to go for it. The first time I ever really got to sit down and talk to Pottz was in a bar in Hossegor, France, when he was drunk. He came up to me and said, "I like you kid, because when you see a lip, you hit it." It was one of the biggest compliments I'd ever had from someone whose opinion I thought was important. It was particularly pleasing because it was good to know I had Pottz's approval.

Tom Curren's influence on young American surfers in the 1980s cannot be overstated, and it was particularly so for me. With Curren every move made sense. There were limits to how radically he was prepared to surf in competition, and he seemed almost safe compared to Pottz, but even in his conservatism he was artistic. If people had called me a Curren clone back in my early days, I would have been nothing but flattered.

Another huge influence in my early days was Mark Occhilupo. He crossed my radar after winning the first professional event at Jeffreys Bay in South Africa in 1984. The Aussie's surfing scared me at first because it was so different. It was like he knew something no one else knew—almost alien. You'd look at his style and wonder where the hell he picked that up from! He held his hands low and pointed them where he wanted to go on the wave. His position on the board seemed so perfect and balanced that he couldn't be pushed off; his legs were in a super-wide stance, but they were delicately poised together. He came back East for a contest soon after that and was beaten in the semis by Shaun Tomson. I was astounded because, at that moment in time, I didn't think he could be beaten. Occy's career moved in strange ways, but his comeback was the greatest our sport has known, and I cheered as loud as anyone when he succeeded me as world champion in 1999.

Matt Kechele (former pro surfer, shaper, mentor):

I probably first started noticing him hanging out at Third Street North in Cocoa Beach. His mom used to work at the Islander Hut, flipping burgers. Kelly and Sean hung out at the beach 24/7 in the summer. I'd bum french fries off of 'em. At that particular beach there was the Apollo Building, left over from the *Apollo 11* mission, and that was the hangout for all the good local surfers, kind of the energy center. Kelly lived three blocks off the beach just by the Minuteman Causeway. In the winter the Apollo was like a wind block. You could keep nice and warm behind the wall. The building was abandoned, but the Islander Hut was right next to it, this classic Florida snack bar serving burgers and beer. Kelly's dad was always there drinking beers.

[Sean and Kelly] were both excellent surfers—both of them were turning heads—but Kelly had a little more magic about him. He'd do a big off the top and just sprawl out in the whitewater and then somehow spring up like a chicken. That was his trademark. When he came back up, people would just go, oh wow! He was so tiny for his age, you kind of wondered if he'd ever get over five feet. Dick Catri was a local legend in Cocoa Beach, and he had the Shaggs Surf Team going. Dick used to shape some boards, and so he made boards for Kelly and his friends. No disrespect, but they were far too wide; they looked like footballs. My shaping career was just getting off the ground, and I went to Kelly and said, Dude, let me make you a real board. So I started making him some boards under the Quiet Flight label.

At fourteen I finished third in the world juniors

in Newquay, England, which was an under-eighteen event, making me the highest-rated fourteen-year-old surfer in the world. People were expecting big things of me, but I wasn't so sure. Even after two seasons, I still hadn't really come to terms with surfing in Hawaii, home of the best and most consistent waves in the world. But I loved going there so much that if I could have my two weeks there every Christmas, I was prepared to pretty much give up the rest of the year.

In 1984, competing in the "menehune" division at the US Nationals at Makaha, I met some of the surfers who would become my life-long friends, guys like Shane Dorian, Ross Williams, Keoni Watson, Brock Little, and Sunny Garcia. It was over the next couple of seasons on the North Shore of Oahu that I fell in with the crew that would guide me, inspire me, and help turn me into a surfer capable of winning in all kinds of conditions. But those first couple of seasons it was all about the fun.

I was scared of almost everything on the North Shore, so I'd spend a lot of time surfing the Ehukai Beach Park, which is mostly sand bottom and smaller. Slowly I ventured along the beach toward Pipeline and started picking off three-footers at the end, while Ronnie Burns, Tom Carroll, Derek Ho, Dane Kealoha, and Johnny Boy Gomes were getting eight-foot barrels. It was a wonderful learning period, and also I met Benji Weatherly, Jack Johnson, and the whole Johnson and Hill clans, who would become my North Shore surrogate families.

Matt Kechele:

I picked Sean and Kelly up from the airport and took them to Mark Foo's house. They were pretty impressed about staying there and meeting the [big wave] legend. It was Kelly's first time in Hawaii, and he was such a puss. It's funny when you look back. I'd take him to spots like Marijuanas or Left-overs, the easier waves. I'd get in as much time as I could at the good spots, and then I'd take them somewhere where they felt comfortable. It was a good thing for Sean because he was that little bit older and more confident, and he could make fun of Kelly, like, C'mon Kelly, man up! I had to cook dinner for them, and our favorite meal was nachos. I'd make this giant pan and we'd just go for it almost every night. Kelly's diet wasn't so good back then. It made you wonder if that had anything to do with his growth. He just loved french fries.

Benji and Jack were even younger than me, but they were already charging Pipe. They loved those days when it was kona winds and Pipe was twelve feet and no one was out. I was terrified because the conditions were so unfamiliar, and it was like you wipe out, you die! They thought it was fun; they were just playing in their sandbox. All the while Brock Little would be somewhere close by, calling us pussies if we didn't pull in.

'86 US Amateurs, Sebastian Inlet.

Taking advice from coach Bruce Walker at the 1986 World's, Newquay, England.

Velzyland,
North Shore,
O'ahu.

Recently, over the past few years

I've had the good fortune to be involved in a Quiksilver video series known collectively as *Young Guns*. For this I traveled to some of the best surfing locations in the world with a group of the hottest young surfers, including France's Jeremy Flores, California's Dane Reynolds, Hawaii's Clay Marzo, and Australia's Ry Craike and Julian Wilson. It was set up so that I was the teacher and they were the students, but it was most definitely a two-way street. To be a good teacher you must never stop learning, and to be around these guys and not have your eyes opened to what is possible, well, you'd have to be dead or stupid. You watch the rad stuff they do and you can't ignore it. You just have to step up to the plate and and join in!

Working on *Young Guns* took me back to when I was their age, around eighteen, and shooting a movie called *Kelly Slater in Black & White*. A lot of the movie was shot on Tavarua in Fiji, my first trip there and the beginning of a lifelong love affair with the island and the people. One day we shot, Cloudbreak was ten feet, but right in front of the resort, the break they call Restaurants was four to six feet and absolutely perfect. Surfing Restaurants that day was one of the greatest days of my life, and after all these years and experiences I'd still rate it top five. That trip, and more specifically that session, were what I'd looked forward to my whole young life. To top it off, John Freeman, who later found fame with *Crusty Demons of Dirt,* got it all on film.

People have subsequently said that *Black & White* is their favorite movie, but even at that time I didn't think the surfing was exceptional. A lot of the filming was pretty rough and raw, but it did capture some highly emotional moments, like my excitement at surfing against my hero Tom Curren in France, and the thrill of winning my first pro event at Trestles.

More important, I think, it captured that wonderful moment in a person's life when everything is fun and exciting, and the feeling you get in surfing that the moment could just go on and on.

Some sort of media thing at the Wave Pool at Disney in '89 with Sean and our crew.

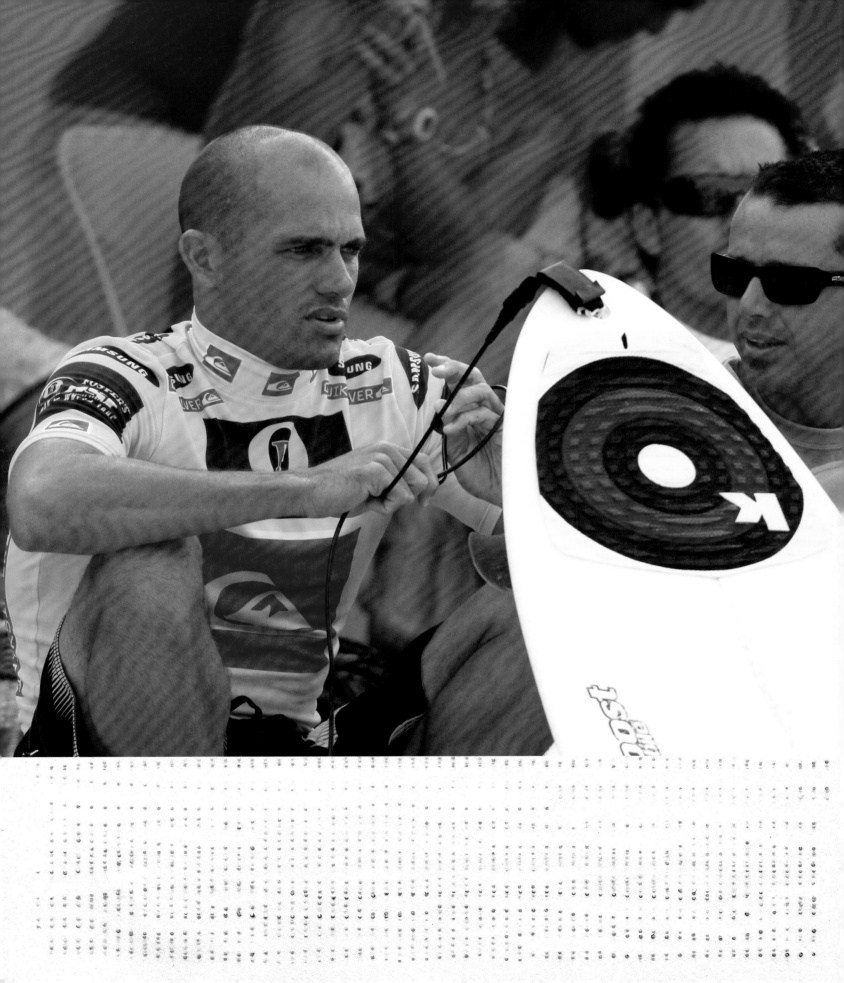

Todd Kline (former top East Coast amateur, Quiksilver manager):

I met [Kelly] when we were both about fourteen, and we spent a lot of time together after that. We hit it off straight away. I hadn't traveled much, maybe a trip to Barbados, so maybe this is a bold statement, but I think I could see almost immediately that he was going to be a world champ. At fourteen he had the talent, style, and charisma of the pros that were in their prime.

He was a smart kid, great at school, yet streetwise, too. He just seemed to make the right decisions. I was a real smart ass, always mixing it up and getting in trouble. Once in a while you could convince Kelly to get into a little mischief. He might have a beer here or there, but he was never the kid vomiting at the party or doing drugs. Our main thing was looking for girls.

I used to spend a lot of time at his house because mine was down south, and central Florida was the epicenter for surfing. I'd either be at Kelly's or at Kechele's. Kech was a mentor to both of us. Kelly's mom always had the door open for me. We spent a lot of time fishing on the backwater. We both came from broken homes where the father did a lot of drinking. Steve [Kelly's father] was around but not at the house. We'd see him at the beach. Judy [Kelly's mother] was raising three kids by herself, and so was my mom. You didn't think much of it then, but now I have the utmost respect for them. It's not easy.

Former Florida teammate and later Quiksilver manager Todd Kline was there at the beginning, and has been close during the last few world title campaigns.

above: Newquay World Titles, '86
opposite: Discussing tactics pre-heat.

35

This is one of the most intimate and close-up barrel shots I think I've ever had and this whole sequence takes place in probably less than a second, but a lot of subtle things happen. In shot 1, I'm leaning forward to get moving and catch up to the lip and set the timing right. I think I'm getting a little on my heel in shot 2, so I'm bringing my shoulder in a little to offset my butt hitting the water. That sets me further up the face so in shot 4 I'm actually looking down the face and adjusting to the changing direction, but I'm also getting stuck a little, which will slow me down. I'll accelerate as I drop down the face coming out of this shot, so I'm getting my hand ready to grab the face as I speed up. The hand in the wave gives me more control and allows me to climb up the face again and avoid falling too low and getting caught up in the tube monster (the turbulence where the lip hits the base of the wave). This was a small enough Cloudbreak day to play with the tube without worrying about getting hurt, just feeling your way through the barrel, testing what can be done in such a small space.

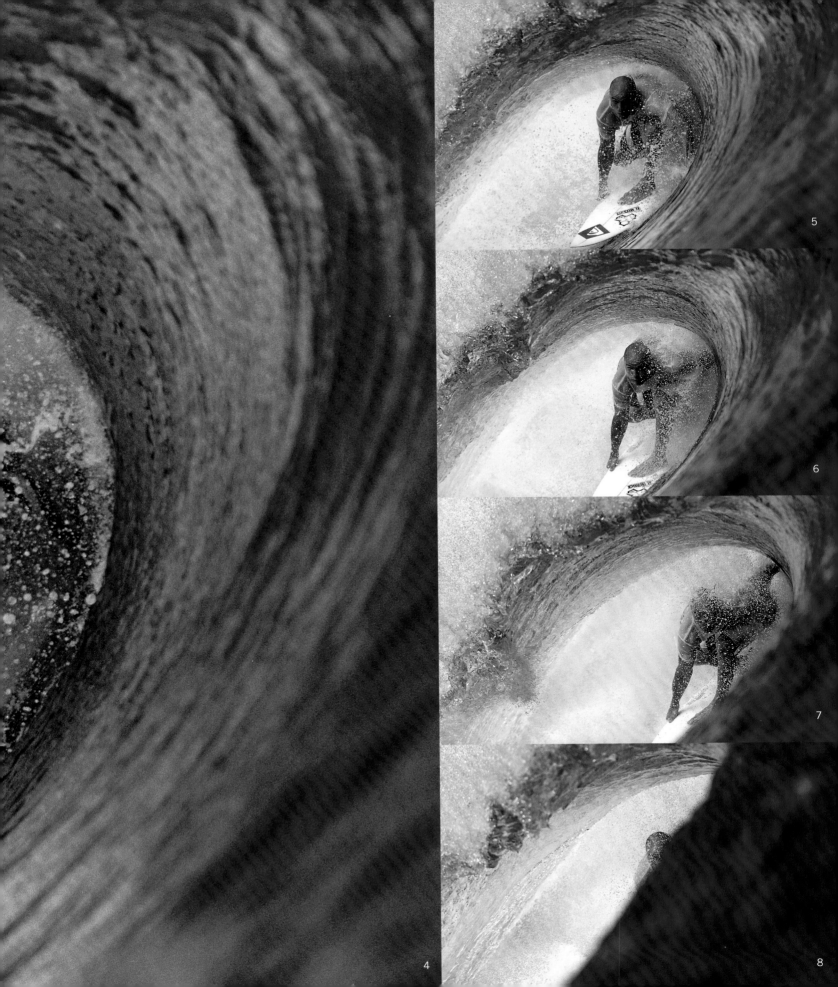

4

5

6

7

8

For the challenge

This is probably just before getting caught inside at Pipe on a big day. If you come over a wave and see the next one breaking, you have to paddle out as far as possible and over toward the channel because you don't want it to push you in too far and have the next one behind it miss the outer reef and unload right on you on the inside reef. If that one doesn't push you too far in, and there's nothing behind it, you're usually fine. It's funny how sometimes you can have a guy right next to you one minute and after the set you can be hundreds of yards apart if one of you just barely gets caught.

You never know 'til you go.

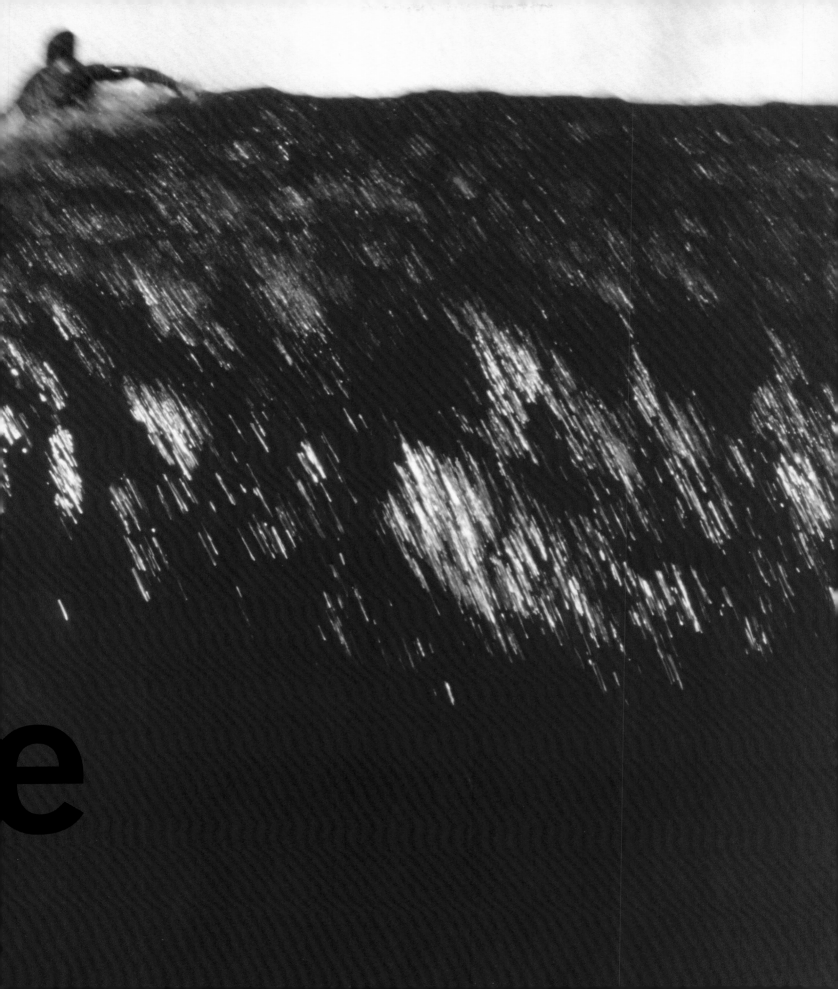

One of my favorite surf shots

is of Michael "Munga" Barry taking off on a twelve-foot peak at Sunset. We were surfing in a heat together and I was about ten feet farther out from him when he turned to catch it. He really needed to get through this heat and was prepared to take a risk, but this was a heavy wave. The wind was blowing about twenty-five knots offshore, and I thought I was way too late to take it, so I paddled over it, looking for the next one. Munga was right behind me, and he flipped around and took off. I couldn't believe it. I thought for sure he just killed himself, but that drop turned out to be one of the great surf photos of all time. I'll always remember how nuts I thought he was to take it, but he made the drop and got a nine-something. He had a nine and a one, and he made it through the heat.

Another time I was talking to Brock Little and he was telling me about surfing Cave Rock in South Africa with Munga. Now Munga never made the pro tour top ten, and some people don't even know his name, but the guy had such wave knowledge and such a knack for finding big, perfect barrels and really charging them. Brock said Munga was on his way out to the lineup and this huge, perfect peak comes. He's way too late on it to make it, but he flips around and stands up and falls out of the sky and eats shit. He paddles back out, and Brock goes, "Why did you do that? You had no chance of making it." And Munga just shrugs and says, "I had to try."

It's that thing, you never know 'til you go. You never know how far you can push things until you do something like that and make it. Almost every wave I've ever made, I've had this thought, I wonder if I could have been a touch deeper, or got a little higher on an air. There's always room for improvement. It's an obsessive/compulsive thing, but it's also what competitors do, what people who are seeking a true challenge do.

I was down in Laguna Beach

one afternoon when I got a call from Chris Malloy. He says they're going to Cortes Bank, the wind is going to be perfect, swell huge. I've been mesmerized by the place since Brad Gerlach, Mike "Snips" Parsons, and Peter Mel got it great. I had to go back to L.A., get my stuff, then get back down to Dana Point to catch the boat late that night. Chris and I got on the boat with photographer Rob Brown and a bunch of guys. We were leaving at midnight, so I grabbed a Del Taco by the marina at Dana Point—the only place open at that time of night and I guess I'm not going to get a Del Taco sponsorship after this! We headed out, and the ocean was calm and beautiful, and I lay down to sleep in one of the gunnels. I started to feel a little queasy, which I can usually handle, but I was getting engine-room fumes as well. I got so sick I had to lift my head up and puke everywhere over the edge about twenty times. When we got out there, all I wanted to do was get off the boat. There's no protection, you can't find still water, there's nowhere to hide. I was feeling so sick back on the boat I thought I might feel better on the big Billabong Odyssey boat, but they had a major sewage issue. It was the most horrid stench of chemicals and poop, so I decided the only thing to do was jump in and surf.

It was small, only ten-foot sets. There were about six Jet Skis, so I took my yellow tow board out and Chris and Shane Dorian were towing me in. This thing kind of jacked up on the reef as I was getting into it. It hadn't looked that big, but it turned out to be one of the biggest of the day. I remember thinking I should pull up into the barrel, but I was too weak to handle the wipeout, so I went straight. In the photo it looks huge. It ended up being a wetsuit ad.

Munga's Sunset late drop.

inset: KS and Chris Malloy tow team, Cortes Bank.

In my early years in Hawaii many of my friends

charged big surf. When Jack Johnson and Benji Weatherly were about fourteen, they were charging second reef Pipe, and even though Jack tends to talk me up and say that I caught on real quick, those guys were surfing bigger waves than me for the first few years I knew them, even though I was a few years older. They just never seemed to be scared.

A bunch of us had quite a few sessions at small- or medium-sized Waimea Bay. Our goal was always to pick a guy, a Waimea regular, and you could not take off in front of him. You had to be inside him. We had all these little games, like "You won't go." That was, any time you're looking down a steep drop at the last second, and the other guy says, "You won't go," then you have to or you're a pussy. It was just a little device to push each other.

Another game was the BDPOC, the Backdoor Paddle Out Contest. The rules were there were no rules. You could grab the other guy's leash and pull him back into the pit, anything to be the first guy to get out past where the waves were breaking. We'd do this instead of paddling out at Pipe where there's sort of a channel, and keeping your hair dry. We'd just make it really tough on ourselves. Taylor Steele would be on the beach filming it, and then we'd all watch the footage at Benji's house that night. It was actually a great way to get comfortable with that section of reef. It made things fun, made a dangerous situation seem lighthearted. In time it helped us understand where the energy of the wave was in relation to the reef, where you had to go on it so it wouldn't hurt you.

above:
Cortes
Bank.

opposite:
Jaws.

When Donny Solomon died

at Waimea Bay in 1995

it was scary because it was so real. He was a close friend and he's gone now, he's not coming back. Was it worth it for that one session? Isn't your life worth more than that? These were the questions that came up continually because we had three friends die in less than three years. I think that period between '94 and '97 woke all of us up. I don't know what effect it had on Brock, who was always the heaviest charger of us all. I think he may have toned it down somewhat because it made it so real for him.

Mark Foo and Todd Chesser were both impressive physical specimens who didn't look like they could be hurt. Chesser looked invincible. He'd do a thousand sit-ups a day and do breathing exercises—getting fit for big waves was his whole deal. And Foo had handled so many closeout situations at Waimea it was unthinkable he could die on a fifteen-foot day at Mavericks.

But then again [former pro and surf writer] Jamie Brisick drowned on a two-foot day at Ventura. He got hit on his head by his board and drowned, and someone revived him on the beach. A firefighter saw him go under and gave him CPR on the beach. So you just never know. More often guys get hurt on the small days. I think all those incidents have made us weigh up the whole deal. What photo, what adrenalin rush, what badge of honor is worth the risk?

For me the answer is to be calculated about it, especially when it gets big. Pay attention to what the buoys are doing, know your lineups really well, and be really focused. I find when you're surfing somewhere like Himalayas, you're so far from the coast that your lineups are up on the hill. You can't see the reef too well either, so you have to pay attention to the boils, the color of the water. You have to ease yourself in; don't just get out there and paddle in deep. What was the biggest wave that came in the last hour, and where did that thing break? What shape was it compared with the smaller ones? When you're surfing an outer reef at twenty-five feet, you're going to need all these evaluations because it's going to break top to bottom. If you get caught inside, you need to know where to paddle to get to where the energy is dispersed more and you can get under it. It's all about calculations.

The late Donny Solomon.

✳✱▼✦╤
★★★★★
★★★★★

I've had a couple hold-downs that freaked me out a little, like two or three different waves, but not to the point where I took any water. I don't think I've been close to drowning, but I have been completely out of breath and scared and really thankful that the wave let up when it did. I've had two like that at Mavericks. On one, I didn't even get caught inside. I caught the first wave of a set and the whitewater of the second one got me. It was a ten-foot day, and I was surfing with [Mavericks pioneer] Jeff Clark. I took off too deep on the only fifteen-footer to come through that day and went straight. I hadn't surfed Mavericks before, and Jeff had told me I couldn't surf in the contest unless I went out and caught a wave on the peak beforehand.

So I flew up there, and that's what I was doing on that first wave when I jumped off and the next one rolled over me. That wave is scary because its energy doesn't seem to dissipate until it goes through the rocks. At the takeoff the wave is already backing off into deeper water, but then it gets shallow again inside and doubles up. Anyway, this thing just picked me up and threw me over the falls and drove me so deep. The problem was I wasn't expecting the hold-down. I'd been through waves nearly twice that size, and there hadn't been too much of an issue. Jeff Clark was on a Jet Ski, and he rode over me twice before I popped up. I paddled back out and caught one more wave to jump back on the horse, but I was pretty shaken up.

It made me understand better what we think happened to Foo. He got his leash caught on the bottom. That's just bad luck and you can't control that. Donny tried to paddle over a twenty-foot wave, and he went over the falls backward. Chesser was the one that really scared me because he was so fit and he wanted it. He wasn't scared of anything, but he took the full energy of a huge wave at Outside Alligator Rock, near Waimea Bay, on the head and then got nailed by maybe ten thirty-foot waves. Derek Ho saw the set as he was driving down the hill, and he said he'd never seen so many waves stacked up. The other guys in the water said they saw Todd come up after the first one, and he just shook his head, dove, and never came up again.

It really shook me up. I remember talking to Shane Dorian afterward, and he goes, "It's not worth it." Then when Malik [Joyeux] died [at Pipe in 2005], that was highlighted again. It was such a freak thing. Sixty guys in the water on an eight-foot day, and it didn't look like that horrible a wipeout from the pictures. Guys do that all day long, but you never know when you're going to hit your head.

The life we lead as traveling surfers, we know thousands of people all over the world, so the odds of a friend dying go way up. That's a horrible reality of the surf community, but one good thing that comes out of it is that we bond together in the face of it.

Cloudbreak foamball.

In this photo I'm on the foamball at Cloudbreak

on what we call an eight-foot wave. You'd probably say it was a bit bigger. All the pros had flown in from Tahiti for the Quiksilver Pro, but there were still two days left prior to the waiting period so they couldn't start the event. We'd seen the swell on the map and flown in for it, but they couldn't run the Pro and [contest director] Rod Brooks was stressing about it. It was just perfect, not a drop out of place.

So many good waves were ridden that day, and I got two that really stood out. One is a Hornbaker shot where Rob Machado is in the foreground paddling out, and the other wave is the one to the right. I remember thinking I was a little too deep but I'd go for it anyway, get a bit of speed going straight off the bottom, and hopefully get a pump or two in there to push me through it. Somebody foamballed it on me, just a little bit, and you can see there's this chandelier of water going through it. I think it was Taj Burrow because I remember him telling me he was thinking about it, but he didn't think it was makeable. From the minute I took off I thought I was going to eat it, then for a second I thought I was going to pull it off. I didn't end up making it, but it was one of the most insane waves I've ever had out there.

Shaun Tomson is probably going to kill me for saying this, but when I was fourteen I was surfing Rocky Rights—the first time I ever went right at Rocky Point because I thought you'd die if you went too close to the rocks—and I saw Shaun take off on a wave with a perfect little barrel section in front of him. He was going to have to backdoor it, but he pulled through the back of the wave instead. I was dumbfounded because I would have given anything for that wave. He must have judged he couldn't make it, but I thought he could have made it for sure.

It wasn't until I got a little older and saw footage of Shaun riding on the foamball that I understood what he did. I guess, being from Florida, I was more about maneuvers than barrels, although I did a lot of dreaming about barrels. On a good day at Sebastian Inlet we'd try to do turns in the barrel like Cheyne Horan. We didn't realize those turns had a purpose; we just wiggled away like we thought Cheyne was doing. Now I look at that early footage of Shaun at Backdoor and Off The Wall, and his barrel riding was so far beyond what anyone else was doing at that time. He was getting as deep on single fins as most guys get on thrusters today.

Shaun coined the phrase "time stands still when you're in the tube," and while I don't fully buy into that, I understand the feeling—when you become so keenly aware of one thing that's happening, and you become so focused that it appears to be happening in slow motion because you notice things peripherally. You see so much more.

There's also a deprivation of the senses. I couldn't even tell you what it sounds like. My ears turn off when I'm in the barrel. When I sit here talking about it, I can't conjure up the sound. I can tell you about what it feels like when my fingers touch the face of the wave, and what I feel in my feet when the wave is pulling at my board. I can tell you what it feels like as I load up the energy in my body and move more into a crouch as I move up the face of the wave. I like to think of tube riding as like a cheetah or a lion hunting its prey. Your body is moving very fast, but your head doesn't move; it stays in one place. It's really about maintaining that focus and that position as you work out what the wave is going to do next. If it's a really square barrel and the lip is coming straight down, then you're going to feel the shock. If it's more of an almond and it pitches out more on the face, it's not going to send this turbulent whitewater up toward you, so it's a little easier to ride deep.

Mundaka. This shot was taken the day Shane and Lisa Dorian had their baby, Jackson. I slept in the car until the tide got low enough to surf, having arrived in France the night before and barely slept. It was crowded but even getting just one wave like this is worth the drive down from France. Pretty cool that the rainbow showed up in the barrel. Gold at the end of that one.

Sometimes the whole wave will cascade in on itself, and you'll have chandeliers of water falling in on you. At those times you don't want to move at all. Your line must be set so you don't have to rely on your fins pushing against the turbulence. In the most intense situations inside the barrel, you need to stay really calm, not react to the wave, just stand on your board and wait. There's a line where you have to move from reacting to the situation to not reacting anymore. It's a space where you have to trust what you've done and let it do its work.

I think every surfer has a best barrel story, and here's mine. The first one I ever got spat out of. It was at Sunset Point on a four- or five-foot west swell, and I was surfing with Matty Liu, who was renowned for dropping in on his friends. At Sunset on a west swell you can get a hollow section out there, but it can be hard to line up. A wave came and we both paddled, and Matty dropped in on me. The thing ledged up and started to barrel, and I was in there behind him. The only choices I had were go straight or pull into the barrel. Matty pulled off the top at the last second, so I pulled up into the barrel. It wasn't a very big wave, but it was double overhead for me at the time, and I was scared. It was the first time I'd felt the wave breathe me in and then just blow me out at the end. I came out of it with my arms in the air, double claiming it! I'm sure I'd had plenty of barrels before that one, but that was the first time I really experienced the feeling. I was fourteen.

**W
A
V
E
S

Y
O
U

C
A
N
N
O
T

M
A
K
E**

I think a lot of people go through a period

where they take off on waves they know they can't make. The difference is whether it's a one-foot wave or a fifty-foot wave. I was the closest guy to Flea Virotzko when he took off and freefell on that now-famous wave in the Eddie contest in 2004. I was twenty feet from him when he landed in the bowl. He stood up on that wave knowing there was zero chance he was going to make it. It was a forty-foot face, and he kept paddling into it knowing there was no possible chance. I think that making an amazing wave is something that you remember forever, and so do the people who see it, but wiping out on an amazing wave is something that everyone remembers, too.

The late Jay Moriarity's wipeout at Mavericks is arguably the greatest single wipeout of all time, and Flea's is right up there with it. But you know what? They both popped up and paddled back out. Flea went over the falls on the next one, too. He walked away that day. He was doing something that was life-threatening, but he had the confidence to pull it off. Sometimes I'll paddle out at Pipeline and feel invincible for maybe half an hour, and then I'll come off the adrenalin high and start talking to people, start getting distracted. At other times I'll start out distracted and grow to think I'm invincible. Either way, it doesn't last forever and you can't rely on it. THAT is stupidity.

Shaun Tomson (world champion surfer, tube rider):

When you look at the evolution of riding the tube— starting back with Conrad Canha and Sammy Lee at Ala Moana, through to the early Pipe guys like Butch Van Artsdalen and Jock Sutherland, then to Gerry Lopez—I think there was a significant shift when I came along because I broke the straight line and did maneuvers in the barrel. I was also the first guy to really ride the tube backside at Pipe. Sure, there were guys cranking a big bottom turn and hoping for the best, but there was no backhand technique. I think what Kelly brought to surfing was a backhand technique for riding the tube. He picked up what I started and moved it forward. His drop-knee, grab-rail style was a big departure from what I was doing. The thing about tube riding that 99 percent of surfers, even the great ones, don't understand is that it is a mental technique. It's all about intuition, controlling time and space. Kelly has mastered all of that. He operates in the tube in a rarified place, way ahead of the pack.

He's going a lot faster than I went. My boards were double concave, similar to what the guys are riding today, but the multi-fin setup enables him to generate that much more speed. He drives the board in the barrel. When you look at other great frontside tube riders like Joel Parkinson, Mick Fanning, and Andy Irons, you'll see that the front foot is flat, the back foot is cocked. The front foot is planted over the concave and the back foot is used to maintain the pressure on the inside rail. But when your foot is positioned like that, there is no rail-to-rail control; you're just maintaining a trim. Kelly's feet are generally flat on the board, and he drives rail to rail. For him, time is expanded in the tube because his greater control allows him to react quicker. And he's only getting started. When he leaves the competitive cycle, I think we're going to see the most creative surfing of his career.

The Eddie is such an important

part of Hawaiian surfing. Eddie Aikau is arguably the second-most-important figure in Hawaiian surfing behind Duke Kahanamoku. He oversaw hundreds of rescues and taught so many people how to save lives, before losing his own so tragically in 1978 while trying to save his crewmates. He'd have to be one of the most respected watermen of all time. The event carries all that tradition with it, and to paddle out there at the Bay and be included in that list of great watermen is a huge honor. To win

Opening ceremony for the Eddie.

it made me feel like more a part of the community. I spend quite a lot of time just wandering around at that event saying hello to guys I've looked up to all my life, and then there are the friends who've passed away riding big waves, and their spirit is there, too.

The year I won it I was in the first heat of the day, and I was the first one into the lineup. A set came through about twenty feet plus. I was right on the spot to take off, but I didn't know if the heat had started. It was the first time I'd been on the peak at Waimea by myself, and it really tested me because I had to rely totally on my own knowledge of the lineup. I flipped around and took the wave, the first of the event. It was only later that I realized how special that was. A beautiful offshore morning with a twenty-foot swell and you're the only one sitting on the peak.

Dropping
down
a
clean
Waimea
face,
Braden
Dias
in
mixed
minds.

This sequence is from the Teahupoo event the first time I won there in 2000.
I think this is the final against Shane Dorian on a day that was more surfable
than your typical barrel feast. This one sort of pitches, I get a little stuck in
shot 3 and I'm trying to stabilize as I go straight down in free-fall in shot 4.
By that point I needed to be on top of my board and judging how far it's
going to throw me and where it'll let me land. My legs are compressed as
I get airborne, and then instantly I have to stretch to stay attached to my
board. I remember landing this one quickly and riding straight out, surprised
that I made it so cleanly. In shot 6, the lip is hitting my shoulder,
and by the last shot I'm already clear and ready to turn again.
You can see the surprise in my body language at the end.
In fact, if I just saw the last shot by itself, I'd be
wondering why I'm just standing there with this
slightly goofy stance.

5

6

7

8

For the money

My
life
as
a
pro
surfer.

Claiming
a
sixth
world
title,
Pipeline
Masters,
1998.

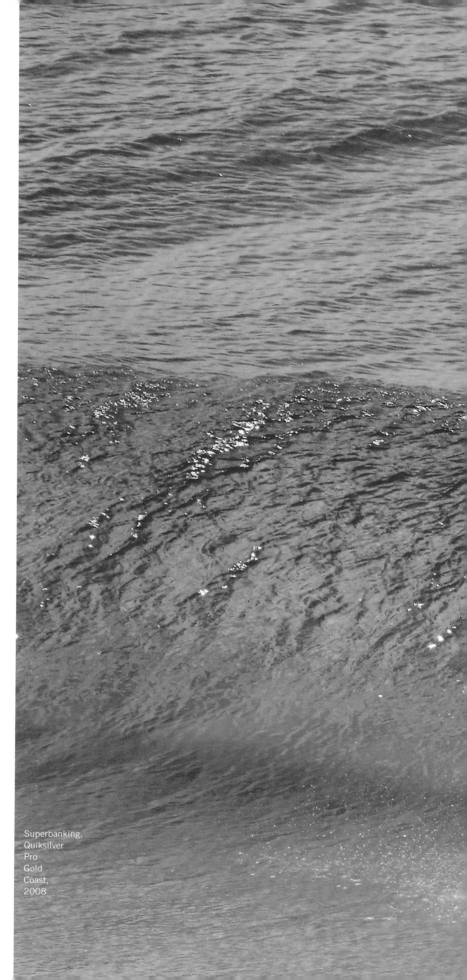

I think it's actually easier to become a good surfer if you start in small, slow waves. In Florida the waves are small and slow, but they break farther from the beach than they do in most places in California, so you get longer rides. I felt that it was easier for me to translate my skills from those waves to bigger and faster waves, rather than the other way around.

If you're from Florida, you graduate to the Caribbean, which these days is not all that exciting for me unless there's a massive swell. A kid from Hawaii going there would be the same, but for me as a kid, everywhere was an adventure.

Superbanking,
Quiksilver
Pro
Gold
Coast,
2008

There are two events that I consider

consider announced my arrival as a pro. The first was the Body Glove Surfbout at Trestles in California on the 1990 Bud Tour, and the second was the Rip Curl Pro in Hossegor, France, in 1992, when I beat Australia's Gary Elkerton to take my first ASP Pro Tour victory. They were both huge stepping stones for me, equally important and exciting. At Trestles I was up against all the best guys in the States, and the waves were perfect, still the best ever for a contest there. We were getting barreled at Trestles! That was my stepping stone onto the world tour and sponsorship with Quiksilver. I actually signed the deal on the beach during the contest. Then beating Gary Elkerton at Hossegor made me feel I'd really arrived.

Early in my career I made a few brash comments about the level of surfing on tour. I didn't think it was that good. I thought it was quite stagnant and boring. There was a huge gap between what was being done and what could be done, and I thought there was a good chance to win a world title. There were a lot of things changing at that time.

There's always been a certain distance between me and many surfers on tour because I don't drink much and I don't do drugs. There are some guys on tour, if they see me chug a beer, it's like the sun just rose. They get so excited, like, "Wow, he's one of us!" It's really not that big a deal—I'll chug a beer once in a while, but it's not my lifestyle. It's not what I really enjoy doing. I don't like feeling bad in the morning. I watched my dad getting drunk every day, and I don't understand the appeal. But everyone has to cut loose once in a while, let some steam off, and if you can't do that mentally and emotionally, you have to do it physically.

None of the American guys I started with—Ross Williams, Shane Dorian, Taylor Knox—really raged that much. We didn't have any big vices. We surfed. The Aussie guys partied a lot, especially the older crew.

The surfing of the older guys didn't scare me. What scared me was the idea of who they were—the Pottzes and the Kongs. The gnarliest competitor was Robbie Bain from Australia, far and away. He'd paddle right at you, look you in the eye, splash water at you, anything. But the funny thing was it made me realize how scared he was. It didn't make me think he was a gnarly guy; it made me think he was terrified of losing. Once I realized that, I didn't let him faze me.

I learned a lesson at Sunset early on. I went out and partied the night before the event, drank way too much, and someone woke me up early and told me the contest was on and I had to surf in the first heat. I ran down to the beach, and the waves were tiny on the point. It was forecast to come up, but I had to surf it really tiny. I got through, went home and rested, and came back and it was six feet. By the semis it was eight to ten, and I kept thinking, lucky I got out of bed and surfed that first heat. It was a perfect swell with a bit of north in it, so you could ride a smaller board, and I probably got the best wave I've ever ridden at Sunset that day. Shane Dorian won that contest and I got third, but the lesson I learned was that you have to focus on the whole event, no matter what the conditions are like.

John Shimooka (former pro surfer)

I met Kelly properly for the first time in 1984 at the US championships in Makaha. He was smaller than me. You look at him now and go, How the hell could that be? But he was. He was just this tiny little kid ripping it up. The media attention was nothing like it is now, but you could definitely see that he was a standout. He was twelve, and I was almost fifteen, and he was right up there with us.

Sunny and I were like one and two in Hawaii, and to get beaten by this little shit from the East Coast at Makaha . . . well, that would have been a nightmare, but luckily we were in different age divisions! Kelly let his surfing do the talking, very quiet but friendly. He just looked like he was having fun.

I don't think we understood "phenomenon" that early in the piece, but he was something else. The way he drew a line on the wave at that age was incredible. Kelly flowed from one maneuver to the next, very much in control. To think on it now, the first hint of the best surfing we're going to see in our lifetime, it gives you chicken skin.

Rod Brooks (contest director)

We were running a split bank at Fistral [in the 1986 world amateur championships] and 84 fifteen-minute heats a day, running for ten hours. At the end of his heat, Kelly remained in the water for nine minutes into the next heat. Finally he took off on a wave, got to his knees, and did an "el rollo," or 360-degree tumble, which one of the judges deemed to be an "up after," or standing to ride a wave after the heat is over. We went through a pretty fiery process in the judging stand, but the judge who called it would not change his opinion. I was left as contest director to uphold the rule book, and Kelly got eliminated from that division, which was the seniors. This caused no end of anxiety for the US team and Kelly in particular, so our relationship got off to a pretty rocky start. [Kelly notes: I just saw Rod as an Aussie who didn't want me to win no matter what!]

His coordination was a pleasure to watch, weight on both feet and total control on his turns, perfect balance above his feet, and the ability to put full weight on his turns. He had natural weight adjustment over the middle of his board down so well. That still strikes me today.

With golf buddies John Shimooka (left) and Pat O'Connell (center).

I had focused all my ambition on winning a world title

in my first full rookie year, 1992, and after France it looked like I could do it. In fact, I wrapped up the title in Brazil, when Sunny Garcia, the last contender with a chance of catching me, lost. I was ecstatic, of course, at twenty the youngest world champion in pro surfing history, but we still had to finish the season with the most serious event of the year, the Pipeline Masters.

I felt I'd proven myself with a gutsy showing at Pipe the previous year, but I was still determined to win the world title with style. I made the four-man final, but it was a bittersweet moment because Sunny Garcia was in the lead when halfway through the heat he was hurt and sent to the hospital with a concussion. With about two or three minutes left, the absent Sunny was still in the lead, and I needed a relatively low score of three or four to win. It was me, Pipe local Liam McNamara, and Australian Barton Lynch, and Liam starts telling me let's block Barton and bring the title back to Hawaii. Not only did I take offense at that personally, but Liam then says that he's in first place. I knew that wasn't right, but I didn't know if it was tactics or if I'd heard wrong. So I said okay, if you want to bring it back to Hawaii, let's neither of us catch a wave and let Sunny win it. He goes, no, we need to block Barton. I was in the lead! I wasn't going to do that. I may have stopped catching waves and let Sunny win it, but that wasn't what Liam had in mind. So a small wave came through and I took it. I caught a piece of crap and beat a guy who was lying on a stretcher. I had mixed emotions about it, but I had won my first Pipeline Masters and my first world title.

Friend and rival Rob Machado makes Pipeline look casual.

In 1995, I really learned what it was

to fight for a world title. Rob Machado had won three events, Sunny had won a couple, and I'd won one before getting to Pipeline. We were the three front runners going into Brazil, then we had a month off before Pipeline. I already knew the scenarios. If Sunny got ninth, I had to win. If Rob got third or better, then even a win wouldn't get me there.

Occy [Mark Occhilupo] was on his comeback trail and had a wildcard into the event, and he met Sunny in the third round right before my heat. It was all lefts that day, which favored Occy. His strategy was to not go after the biggest, craziest ones; it was to get the medium-sized ones and just get the job done. Sunny admits that he's way better at Backdoor than on the lefts, and when the rights aren't happening, he really shows his frustration. So that's what I was hoping for. Everything fell apart for Sunny. He broke his leash on a wave that wasn't that big and had to swim. Meanwhile, Occy was getting good scores. I was getting ready for my heat and wasn't watching, when the crowd lets out this roar. I turned around expecting to see Sunny, but it was Occy just finishing up. I figured for Occy to get a roar like that against the hometown hero, it must have been a really good wave.

Now Occy is starting to stress out because there had been such a campaign for Sunny to win the title, and Sunny himself was talking it up, saying stuff like, "If this was a horse race, I wouldn't bet against me." Occy was seriously worried he was going to get jumped. There's two or three minutes left, I'm paddling out, and suddenly it looks like Occy is going to purposely drop in to get scored an interference and give Sunny the heat. As I got closer I realized he wasn't doing that, but he was talking Sunny into them. He's going, "Take this one . . . go!" He obviously knew that he was putting Sunny's world title hopes on the line, but there was nothing he could do. The heat was over, and Sunny was out of the event and the title race.

Why the Pipe Masters is the most exciting contest in the world for spectators. KS center stage.

Now the pressure was back on me. We were all old childhood friends—me, Sunny, and Rob—but this had split our friends into three camps. Rob and I had the same manager, we played music together, and now we were going for the world title together. It had just started to get a little strange between us. We were on the same side of the draw, so we ended up in the semifinal together. If he wins, he's world champ. If I win, I have to go on and win the final. We did rock, paper, scissors for the first wave. I think I won, but it was a flawless, peaky day. It was pretty obvious that if the right wave came, he'd go left and I'd go right. I think Backdoor generally outscores Pipeline, but this was one of those days where you could get tens going either way. I think that heat was a true celebration of surfing in a competitive environment. It was a release of a lot of unspoken things between us. Little things had been building up. I won the heat, and Rob congratulated me on the beach, knowing that his title hopes were still alive. I don't remember him wishing me luck in the final though!

Now I had to get past Occy. I didn't know how he was going to approach the heat, but I could see the stress on his face, so I paddled over to him and said, "Occ, you know how much winning this means to me, but it means just as much to you." I meant it as a friendly gesture, and he did seem more relaxed after that. Then I went out there and won the heat. My friends carried me up the beach, and I was the world champion again.

I won the world title in 1998 in similar circumstances against Australians Mick Campbell and Danny Wills. Mick and Danny both went out [of the event] early at Pipeline, and I had to place third or better to win my sixth title. I ended up in the quarterfinal against Rob again, and the surf was similar, six to eight feet and going both ways. Rob knew the situation. He could fuck me up, or he could lay down and do a disservice to all the Australians. I don't think he felt any loyalty to them, but no doubt he felt a loyalty to surfing. He had to go out there and do his job. So I went out and won the heat, and only afterward did he tell me what had happened. He'd called his older brother Justin, who's a really competitive guy, and asks, "What do I do?" And Justin says, "Rob, you go out there and you kick his ass."

When we got to the beach at the end of the final, all our friends were there and they carried both of us up the sand. It was an amazing feeling, but I really felt for Mick and Danny, who were on the beach with their families. They were a real team, at number one and two in the world that year leading into Hawaii: they worked together, trained together, traveled together, and were so totally motivated to win. But it wasn't to be.

So many great surfers have missed out on world titles, going way back to Cheyne Horan, Simon Anderson, and Gary Elkerton. Most surf fans in the world and probably most guys on tour believe that Taj Burrow has enough natural ability to win a world title. Whether he has the confidence and the competitive ability, I don't know. So far he's been close but it's yet to be seen.

Some people in life just have this belief that it belongs to them and they are going to take it. I've always had that belief, but I've not always verbalized it. Andy Irons, more than anyone in recent years, has made it real clear that he believes it. Tom Curren was much more subtle about it, but I know that Tom believed those titles were his. Some people are aggressive about it, some more submissive. I tend to be on the less aggressive side, but that doesn't mean I believe it any less. Taylor Knox is arguably the best frontside carving surfer of the modern era, but there are certain areas in his surfing that he's had to work on. The most notable is his backside tube riding, and he's done a great job on that in the past couple of years. He's also had to work on aerials, and he's still not known as an aerialist. You need to be able to bust a big air reverse when you're behind in a heat. Taylor is a beautiful, carving power surfer, much like Tom Carroll, who could never bust an air. In Tom's era you could win world titles that way; you probably can't anymore.

Rob Machado finished runner-up a couple times. I don't think most people realize how competitive Rob is, but he grew up with an older brother beating him at everything. He's a freaking competitive guy, and he had the natural ability to win a world title, but maybe he didn't want it enough. Who can put their finger on exactly what that thing is? And in practical terms, it might just mean that they didn't have the luck.

The moment I won my semi at Pipe in '98 and knew I had just won my 6th title.

Fast forward now to 2003, when I lost at Pipeline to Andy Irons. That loss was one of the most grueling processes I've been through in my life. I really learned what it was like for Sunny, Rob, Mick, Danny, Shane Beschen, and all the guys who had come so close. In '03 my seventh world title was within my grasp. If I hadn't broken bones in my foot and missed out on the Fiji event, I might have already had the title, but it came down to the last day at Pipeline. It was Luke Hitchings, Joel Parkinson, and Andy Irons in the semifinal, and Luke got one of the best waves of the contest, but he had only one good wave. Andy had a couple of okay waves, and Joel looked to have convincingly won the heat already. Andy had to hold Luke off from getting a second wave and putting him out of the title race.

It was so close, but that second wave never came for Luke. It was my dad's birthday. He'd passed away just the year before, and I'd overcome the emotion of all that and had one of my greatest years performance-wise, to get all the way to this point and have the bubble burst. I remember sitting in my house afterward thinking, I can't imagine a worse feeling than this . . . at least in my career. It really gave me empathy for those other guys and allowed me to grow a lot. I mean, there's so much ego involved. I was hearing stuff like, He's not as good as he was. The other guys are passing him by—all that kind of mumbling was going on, and it was weighing on my mind.

The fact is, losing allowed me to grow so much as a person, and that allowed me to come back in 2005 and win. By the time I was the champion again, I understood myself and my competitors so much better, and I felt so much more comfortable in different situations. And I was able to respect people, not just as competitors or surfers, but as human beings and friends.

Taylor Knox (pro surfer, friend)

That was a biggie for him, losing in '03, no question about that. He felt the whole world was against him. Of course, surfing is not the whole world; it's like a grain of sand. But when you're in the middle of it, it can seem like the whole world. You have to ask yourself, if I broke my legs and couldn't surf, would that mean I was half a man? Surfing isn't who you are, it's just something you do.

Kelly should be appreciated by all the other competitors for where he's taken surfing. We could have had a world champion who just went off the rails and got a ton of bad press. Instead we got a guy who just makes us all glow.

above: A picture worth a thousand words. Losing ain't easy. Pipe, '03.

opposite: Winning, on the other hand, is pretty good. Bells '08.

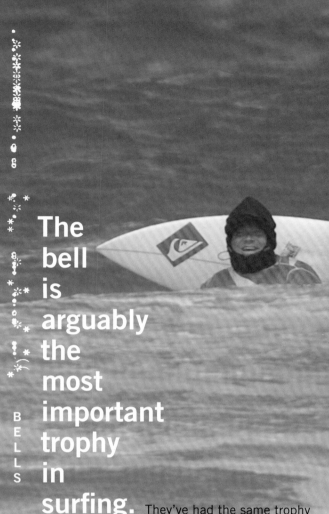

The bell is arguably the most important trophy in surfing.

B E L L S

They've had the same trophy since the very beginning, and it's withstood the test of time. One bell goes out every year, so there are thirty-five people in the world now who have one. I won the bell in 1994 for the first time on my third time there.

I've never been a huge fan of the wave at Bells Beach, on Australia's blustery southern coast, but it is challenging and it's such a great amphitheater to watch surfing from. It's not an easy wave to surf because it goes from being somewhat steep at the takeoff to running down the line and being hard to judge, to flattening out in deeper water and then closing out in the shorebreak. It's a wave with a lot of different faces, and you need to find a board that rides like a shorter board but that you can carve on. I think the trick to Bells is not doing deep bottom turns. You've got to surf more up on the face. The steep part of the wave doesn't start until at least halfway up the face, whereas a wave like Teahupoo or Pipeline is so steep that you can't even get up the face, so you have to turn on the bottom. Bells is so flat that if you initiate a bottom turn, you'll lose all your speed by the time you get to the top.

In 2005, I was eating dinner at the Surfrider Café in nearby Torquay and looking at their collection of photos of Bells over the years. There's a particular photo of Wayne Lynch doing a backside turn, and I realized that he wasn't turning off the bottom, he was up the face. I thought, my God, I've surfed here all these years, and I've only just now figured out that you can't surf the bottom of the wave. The other thing is you can't surf under the lip. You have to surf in front of it, which is how I approach Jeffreys, a running wave where if you hang with the lip, you don't utilize the best part of the wave. Bells isn't as steep or fast as Jeffreys, but when it's really good, as it was in 2006, it can be similar.

I wasn't even going to surf the Bells contest in '06. I was thinking about retiring, and I was really quite serious about it. I was going to surf a few events, and Bells wasn't one of them. But just before the contest I checked the maps and saw all of this swell that was going to hit, and I realized that this could be the greatest year ever. The previous year there'd been nine lay days in a row. I'd stayed in Sydney surfing great ten- and twelve-foot waves up and down the coast, while everyone was sitting down there in one-foot onshore slop. I was talking to Taylor Knox every morning to get a report, and he was getting so frustrated that I was getting all the surf. There was a picture of me on the front page of one of the papers with the headline, "To hell with Bells, I'm surfing the Sydney storm." I mean, as if I'd say that! That was such a bad year, not a single heat was run at Bells, the first time in thirty-five years that had happened.

Clean
face
cutback
at
Winkipop.

Mark Richards (4x world surfing champion)

I lost a lot of times, but when it really mattered, I was the one who was fortunate enough to win. With Kelly, I think it was very revealing the time he just missed out on the title [in '03], and there was a video of him crying in the shower. I think it was his brother who said, This is the first time Kelly hasn't won what he set out to win, the first time he'd lost something that really meant something to him.

I had this advice, and I was determined to give it. I said, How serious are you about winning the title this year? He said he really wanted it. I said, Well, you have to pull back on the Hollywood stuff. You lost the Quiksilver Pro because you went off to hang out with big-titted blondes at the MTV Awards. If you're serious, you've just got to put that shit on hold. I explained my feeling that the whole game plan had changed. The other guys weren't in awe of Kelly anymore, they thought they had his measure, and they did unless he was completely focused.

But 2006, everything was lining up just right. I had the board that I'd won on at Jeffreys Bay the year before, when I probably put in my best performance in an event ever, so I felt really confident on it. On the final day I was already into the quarters, but they still had a few heats to run of the previous round, so Joel Parkinson was going to have to surf four times if he made the final. And at this point I had never beaten Joel man on man. He made it into the quarters.

There was a really interesting quarter between Occy and Andy Irons. Now you wouldn't really expect Occy to beat Andy these days, and Andy was on his game, but Occy was perfectly in sync. Andy was sitting out the back with priority, and Occy needed 8.9 to win the heat, with maybe seven minutes left. This giant set comes as the Jet Ski is taking Occy back out; he jumps off, scrapes over the first one, and is sitting there for the second. Andy's too far inside but Occy's in the perfect spot. Andy has priority, and all he has to do is take off, but it was barreling at triple overhead when it got to him, so there was nothing he could do. Occy took it and scored a 9.9 and won. He ended up in the second semi against Parko [Joel Parkinson].

I happen to think Occy is the best surfer ever at Bells, and one of my dreams was to beat him in a final there, but beating Parko man on man for the first time would be equally satisfying. As it turned out, it was Parko.

73

Everyone listening online to the Bells event in '08 probably got brainwashed by the commentators saying I was crazy for paddling up to Rincon toward the end of the heat. I'd seen a few come through, even before the final, and with the tide rising, waves dropping, and Bede Durbidge sitting in the bowl with priority, I was sure my options looked better up the point. I caught one little one that didn't pan out, and as I paddled back out, a good one came through but I was out of position. Two waves later I caught one and started it with an air. That put the heat back in my hands, along with my third bell. I was pretty stoked when I climbed onto the Ski. I'd told my girlfriend I wasn't going to waste our trip by not winning, and it came true. :)

RIPCURL PRO
WORLD CHAMPIONSHIP TOUR EVENT

SURF & MUSIC FESTIVAL
BELLS BEACH, TORQUAY
LIVE WEBCAST ON RIPCURL.COM

The tide was getting high, and the waves were flattening out a lot. The swell was dying a little and the wind was picking up, making it really hard to surf. My strategy was to get out there and get the first good wave that came along. With the tide filling in fast, there might not be another one. A big set wave appeared, and I could see it had a lot of steep face on it. I came off the bottom on the first turn, snapped off the top and disappeared. Second turn I did the same kind of thing, and third turn there's this big close-out wall, and I'm thinking, should I carve this thing or hit the lip? If I hit the lip, it's going to pitch me out, and with so much wind I wouldn't be able to control my board. So I made that split millisecond decision and did this big grab rail carve all the way to the bottom, and when I got there, there was still a little more curve on it, so I carved it around a little more. I was thinking to myself, I got a keeper there, but I couldn't hear the scores. It wasn't until about ten minutes later I heard that I'd got a 9.67, which I think is the best score I ever got at Bells, certainly one of them.

I won the event, went up on stage and grabbed the bell, shook the hell out of that thing, and then the local Aboriginal tribe came up and painted my face with ochre and gave me a didgeridoo. The whole deal was quite magical. I stayed at the site until everyone left, so that I didn't have to run the gauntlet . . . and then I just walked the hundred yards to the car, my bell under my arm.

F O C U S

I think that sometimes I need to have distractions in order to keep me focused, if that makes sense. I need to feel I'm off my game before I really wake up. I think what happened that first contest at Snapper Rocks in '05, and at Bells following it, were what led me to getting focused and winning my seventh title that year. I would never claim they were the reason I won, but they were part of the journey. Both Mark Richards and Bruce Raymond were also important parts of that journey, with their advice to me both personally and professionally. They helped me see things from a different view. Another former pro, Mitch Thorson, also threw me a lot of great stuff that year. As a competitor you have to be open-minded, but also you have to have your own way of doing things.

There was a moment on the Gold Coast when I was struggling, and Bruce sat me down and told me where my surfing was going wrong. That was hard for me because I've always felt that my surfing symbolized much more than just surfing. The choices I make in the water paint a much bigger picture of my life. Bruce gave me the father-to-son talk and told me to simplify things and they'd be better. It was just the right information at the right time because it applied to a lot of things in my life, not just my surfing. When I look back at my career, that was a profound moment.

How sweet it is. Back in the winner's circle with #7. A joyful moment watching Nathan Hedge take out Andy Irons in Brazil in 2005 to hand Kelly the title.

this page, clockwise from top: SL8R, 2006; showering away the tension, Hossegor, France; with Rob Machado at the Pipe Masters; warming up with Taj Burrow after a tense J-Bay final, '07.

Shaun Tomson (former world surfing champion)

It seems there is a trend on the tour to much more upright surfing, a more stiffened lower back, but Kelly is all rubber-like flexibility. There are a few simple words that define the essence of great surfing—maneuvers and techniques have evolved over the last thirty years, but the essential DNA helix of what constitutes truly great surfing is unchanged: speed, power, rhythm, aggression, style, and imagination. Kelly has all this, and he has that little extra chromosome of intuition, a knowingness, a prescient reactivity to the ebb and flow of the ocean. His wave selection is uncanny, and he would select many waves that others would pass up only to have the waves double up through the Impossibles section, the fastest, hollowest portion of the ride. He came smoking on down the line toward me on one as I paddled back out, turning forward for maximum speed, the lip inches from his head, running for the light on his concave, the foamball roiling beneath his feet. He looked calm and unhurried, at the very center of his universe, right where he wanted to be. He smiled, and I smiled back.

I remember someone saying that motivation is temporary, but inspiration lasts forever. That's what I've found as I've moved along in my career, that it's taken more inspiration than anything else. I might have the motivation to beat a rival to get him back for beating me, but that only lasts for that heat. The inspiration becomes more of a spiritual thing, even though competing in a surfing contest seems to be the polar opposite of spirituality, because it's all about gaining for yourself. I've found in recent years that my best results have come when I'm simply inspired to go ride the wave, that I'm just enjoying the act for its own sake and I'd be just as happy for the other guy to win. That's kind of an odd approach because you're there to win.

It's about balance. The more I look at things, the more I realize it's about understanding someone else. When you begin to understand someone else's fears and hopes, their stoke and their excitement, that's when a certain spirituality can come into sport and you can go somewhere beyond competition.

A friend just e-mailed me a quote from Krishnamurti, "When you step away from competition is when you truly grow." It's funny, because right now [September '07], I'm totally engaged in a battle from behind for my ninth world title, but that's the way I feel.

Bruce Raymond (former pro surfer, Quiksilver executive)

When I gave Kelly advice, he knew that there was no agenda, and I think I've been able on some occasions to tell him things that others couldn't. That still applies today. If a promo is bullshit, I'll tell him so, and I'll advise him not to do it. Or I'll say I think you need a coach, or I really don't like the way you're doing this, and he'll listen because he knows it's coming from the right place. A few years ago Mark Warren and I watched him surf on the Gold Coast, and he was doing these big cutbacks and bashing the foam hard. Because of his athleticism, he'd bring it around and come out—big tick for that—but it just didn't look good. Joel and Mick were bouncing off the top of the foam, Kelly was going straight into it. We told him we knew he could do it anyway he wanted to, but this looked better. We advised him to get a coach.

I think the thing that surprised most of us was how long [after his retirement] it took Kelly to get back on top, and I think a turning point in that was when Mark Warren and I confronted him in Queensland. I think the phrase we used was "a pissing contest with the judges." He had some sort of attitude about the judging criteria, which he wanted to change. He was doing very difficult things, but it wasn't great to watch. Then he went down to Bells and was beaten by Bede Durbidge, and he phoned me and said he was over it, that he was considering walking. I told him I thought he should talk to the head judge and ask him what he wasn't doing, work with it and also put them on notice. I told him a story from the early days at Bells when they had a double-decker bus for the judges. It was a perfect day, and after my heat I walked up into the bus just as Shaun Tomson got this incredible wave right to the beach, never put a foot wrong. My jaw dropped because I realized it was impossible for anyone else to win the event. Then the head judge said, "Oh Shaun, same old, same old . . ." And I realized in the next instant that in fact it was impossible for Shaun to win. I told Kelly that story, and then he went to Tahiti and won.

Winning
form
at
Quiksilver
Pro
Gold
Coast,
'08.

Clinching
#8,
Mundaka
'06.

1

2

3

6

7

This is in the semifinals of the '05 Pipe Masters, I think my first wave of the heat. It kind of jumped up, and in the photo you can't really tell, but you don't get a wave much bigger than this at Backdoor. Maybe it's not full second reef, but it's one of those days that I really love, about six to eight foot with an occasional bigger one, a short interval west swell with a little bit of north in it, just chunky A-frame peaks. If you love Backdoor, this is what you look for. That's Kalani Chapman going left. Mick Fanning was in the heat too, and Cory Lopez. When this wave came I just thought, this is the best Backdoor wave I've ever seen. I'm going no matter what! If I go over the falls and die, it doesn't matter, because this is the wave I've waited my whole life to catch. You can see in shot 3 it really starts to jack and then gets square. It's a little steeper in front of me so I'm backdooring the section. In shot 5, it looks perfect and I've set my line right, then I'm into my first pump on a 6'5" and I probably needed something a little bigger. So, out of the pump and set my turn, then there's a chandelier section ahead and I probably didn't turn up into it quick enough. The line I've set is going to put me right where the lip is landing. Had I made it through the initial burst of whitewater, I would have been okay, but I didn't 'cause I pretty much gave up after that in the heat and also got an interference, if I remember right. I didn't really care much after falling on that wave. It will probably always sort of haunt me.

For the hell of it

My
other
life.

Bodysurfing
Pipe.

Mark Cunningham (bodysurfer, guru)

I think most of us were bodysurfers at the very beginning of our wave-riding careers, and I bet Kelly did a bit as a grom in the warm water in Florida. Most people hear North Shore, and they're thinking twenty-foot Waimea or fifteen-foot Sunset, but there are countless two- or three- or five-foot days when you can have the best time without worrying about drowning or breaking your neck. I think Kelly has seen the joy in that, and it may be because of the saturation of board surfing in his life. Another attraction in bodysurfing—and I've noticed this in Machado, too—is that these guys are under such a hot, burning spotlight the minute they set foot on a beach. They walk down there with a board under their arm and every eye is on them. I can't imagine that pressure. The beauty of bodysurfing is that you're not going to bust a mind-blowing air or get the tube of the day. If you get in the pocket for three or four seconds, that's a bitchin' ride. I think part of the appeal is that Kelly can go out in the water and not have to be the top dog, sort of anonymous. That's what I enjoy about it. I'm not performing on the ocean. I'm just in it, just a piece of it, just this little coconut head floating on the surface.

I knew who Jeff Hornbaker was before I met him.

HORNY

I'd seen his photos since I was a little kid, and I knew he'd been to the best surf spots in the world with the best guys. When I actually met him I was pretty new on the international scene, only just getting to the position where the photographers were going to turn their cameras on me.

One day pretty early in the piece, probably '92, we were at Narrabeen [in Sydney] for the Coke contest and the waves were pretty good. I wanted to surf Little Avalon, this reef break right by where I'd just bought an apartment. Horny was living around there, too. That afternoon most of the pros were surfing at Newport Peak, but I wanted to surf Little Av, and Horny wanted me to surf the Avalon beachbreak. We had to get a shot done for Quiksilver, and he goes, "Look, thirty of the best guys in the world are surfing Newport, and I'm here to shoot you, the least you could do is work with me, you little shit."

Maybe not those exact words, but that was the drift. I went, Well, I'm surfing Little Av, and if you want to shoot it, well and good. If you don't, go back to Newport, I don't really care. And I didn't, because this was the first time I'd been there when Little Av was working, and I wasn't going to pass up the session. We got in this argument, back and forth. Finally I told him, "You know what, Jeff? Your ego is too big to deal with the fact that I don't care if I shoot with you or not." He was shocked, like how dare you talk to me that way! Basically, it was two egos going at it. Mine was the young guy who wasn't going to be told what to do, his was all about respect.

The light went behind the hill, so I went down to the beachbreak to make him happy. We both budged a little bit, and from that point on, we've been fine. I called his bluff, and he probably didn't like it at the time, but ever since then we've been really close. He's a deep thinker, a guy who's always seeking the truth, the kind of person I tend to gravitate toward. We've had so many great trips together around the world. We'd often share a cabin on the [Quiksilver] Crossing when one or the other of us was going through a breakup, so there'd be sob stories to share. One time I was going through a difficult period, and Jeff had a book called *Love Without Conditions* by Paul Ferrini, which he gave me to read. Everything in it made perfect sense, and it helped me reach a point of understanding. We got one surf session the whole trip, so there was a lot of time to write and think, to fish and talk.

If you're doing an intimate shot, something posed or artsy, I think it matters a lot how well you know the photographer because you need to know if it looks dumb that no one is going to see it. You have to feel confident if you're going to take chances. Most times if I'm asked to do something a bit out of the ordinary for a photo, I won't do it because I'm worried it's going to turn up somewhere out of context. One thing Jeff has always said is, if you don't like the shot, don't worry, it's safe with me. And he's never once wavered in that.

Turtle Man,
Grand
Turk Island,
2004.

Jeff and I will often do these pictures

with things that we find. Once in the Mentawais a big tree had fallen over, and there was a hole in the middle of it that was big enough for me to climb into. Horny's artistic concept was that I would emerge as if reborn or something. There's this one shot where I'm hiding in there, then I climb out and reemerge into my real self.

Probably the most fun one we ever did was when we were in the Dominican Republic on the Crossing. We'd eaten in a restaurant two days in a row, and there was this huge turtle shell on the wall in the bar. It was fifty years old or something. I said, "Can I buy it?" The guy thought about that for a minute and then asked for a hundred bucks. I don't normally condone buying decorative things made from dead animals, but I figured it had been there a long time, and they weren't going to go out and replace it. It was a beautiful shell, but it wasn't in very good shape. It needed to be lacquered up to bring the colors out, but each of the plates on its back were about six inches across and there were twenty or thirty of them. It was a big shell. From the ground, it came up to my belly button, and the wire they'd used to hang it on the wall fit around my body perfectly. When I put it on, my head stuck out exactly like the turtle's would have. So a while later on Grand Turk Island I put the thing on, and it covered me from my neck to my knees, and it felt just about right. I told Horny I was going to go swim with it, and he should take a picture. When you swam with it, you could feel the perfect hydrodynamics of it, the perfect curve and foil of the shell. You could get a real sense of how a turtle moves through the water. It was such a cool feeling. We shot a sequence of me as a turtle, beaching myself, and then turning around and going back into the water. It was on my thirty-third birthday.

Jeff Hornbaker (photographer, friend)

When you first meet someone, and you're going to work together, you try to get inside their heads somewhat. When I started working with Kelly, he was really an adversary. Now, I don't know if that was because he had to work with me because I worked for Quiksilver, or whether he'd just never been given an order before. But at first we really knocked heads. He thought I was a control freak, and being a free spirit, he didn't like being told what to do. I know about that because it's the way I am, too. I could relate to it, but at the same time, I'm like, you little bastard . . .

It took about a year and a half of others convincing him that I was okay, that I knew what I was doing. I've run into that a lot, where you really have to work to get someone's trust to a point where you can reveal them and things about them. I'd say Kelly was the most difficult subject to get that trust.

Kelly was like a wolf. After he realized that I was going to be there and wasn't going to go away, he decided to try and live with it, and slowly he became comfortable with it, then assertive about it. For my part, I made it known to him that if he didn't feel right about some things, if it didn't feel like him, then don't do it. A lot of times in the creative process you go way out there and end up doing something completely abstract, not what you set out to do at all. Kelly showed a willingness to go out there and cocreate, but at certain times, he'd just be over it and stop and walk away.

Some of the best material comes when you only work about twenty minutes in a day. The creative process unfolds in the moment. It's not so much that I'm a great photographer and he's a great model. It's more that we share the lifestyle that creates those moments you can capture. You're just there observing it, and you can't help getting involved in the creative process. For example, I can't play drums for shit, but if Kelly starts fooling around with a guitar, I'll be belting out a rhythm on something. It's infectious. When we're shooting, Kelly gets involved in the same way, always looking for the next tree to climb or rock to get into. He's a great muse in that sense.

this spread:
Grand Turk
Island, 2004.

S H E L L S

Horny
and
I

have this thing where we both collect shells wherever we are in the world. I think this was in the Mentawais.

above:
Private
jet
to
Paris,
2006.

above right:
Paris,
2006.

left:
Mentawais,
2000.

This was for *Citizen K,* a high-end fashion magazine that does

a lot of edgy, risqué stuff. Unfortunately, it was published! Their idea for the shoot was to have me dress up like a fish out of water, basically—to put me in crazy getups I wouldn't normally wear. The shoot was originally supposed to take place in New York, but at the last minute they told me they had flown a dozen people to Paris because that's where I was. It turned out they all lived in Paris and it was just a pressure tactic to get me there. Anyway, I was supposed to have left Paris that day, but I felt really guilty that they'd spent all this money, so even though I didn't want to do it, I did. Believe me, there were a lot sillier outfits than the one in the picture. They wanted me in a shirt that barely covered me and some really tight underwear, strange looking shoes . . . I just said, you guys are out of your minds. They're like, "But eet is so 'ot! So sexy!"

I have to explain the scene. The photographer knew a little about surfing, so I could connect there. But the fashion editor of the magazine was something else. This guy walks in, and he had kind of a top hat pulled low over his face with a feather sticking out of it, no chin, very tall and thin, and flamboyantly gay. He had on a leopard-print trench coat that went down to his ankles, and when he took that off he had this giant lion's head Prada belt buckle at the top of supertight black slacks, and where his hands fit into his pockets were these jeweled studs in the shape of two six-guns pointing at his package! To top it all off, when he came over to shake my hand, I noticed he had ketchup all over his bottom lip. It was straight out of *Zoolander*. At one point in the shoot, I remember looking at Bruce Gilbert and going, I'm hungover, I'm in the silliest suit imaginable, I feel like a total idiot, and they're getting all of this on camera. It was about as bizarre as it gets, and I look back on it sometimes and wonder how I let myself get into that situation.

THE JAMES DEAN SHOOT

It was for *Interview* magazine.

Bruce Weber knew a friend of mine from Florida who works in the fashion industry, and he wanted to get me for a shoot for something. This was back in '95, I think. Bruce said come by when you're in New York, and we'll shoot a couple different things. It turns out he wants me to do something for Versace, something for *Interview*, and something for *L'Uomo Vogue*, the Italian *Vogue* for men. I get there and there's this naked girl on the set. She surfed a little bit, so Bruce thought she and I would have a nice connection. How this was meant to be I'm not sure, but he throws me straight onto the set with her. I'd never taken a picture with a fully nude girl before, so I was kind of shy, but she wasn't shy at all.

Every time I've worked with Bruce he's been really quick. Quick but thorough. He tries to make you feel comfortable on the set, he plays music that he thinks you'll like, he has food, and for me he had a guitar that I could strum between takes. And then at the end, he'll put his hands together and bow and say thank-you, and you know that's the end, not one more frame. I thought that was kind of cool. I've shot with him four or six times, and he always has an entourage of camera assistants, like six good-looking young guys.

Bruce didn't say anything about James Dean at the time, but I remember when I first saw the shot thinking that there was something vaguely familiar about it. It was only when a friend pointed it out that I began to wonder if it had been intentional. If it was, I take it as a compliment.

opposite:
James Dean look-alike, New York, 1995.

right:
With Rob and Sal, *Surf's Up* premiere, Hawaii, 2007.

SURF'S UP

We were surfing at Trestles

a couple of years back, and some guys said they were going to make an animated surf film. They worked for Sony, and they wanted to interview us and get the real voices of surfers, potentially for this movie. None of us originally were going to be in anything more than a sound byte, but later on the producers contacted me, Rob Machado, and Sal Masekela and said they wanted us to be characters in *Surf's Up*. I thought it was totally cool. My daughter is now eleven, and I thought it would be great for her to see me in it.

Surf movies always try to have a plot that they think is universal, but it never is. It's always this big buildup, like in *Blue Crush*, and it doesn't work. It doesn't speak to average people because they don't surf and they don't get it, and it doesn't speak to surfers because it's so hokey. But in a cartoon you can take all the elements that translate universally and treat them humorously, and that seems to work. It can be young and fun and yet cool enough for older people. You take *North Shore*— the same story line as *Surf's Up*: guy comes from nowhere, doesn't really know how to surf, doesn't quite win the contest, but gets the girl. Now that was the stupidest movie ever, but *Surf's Up* is just great.

Is there anything better?

It's the purest form of surfing, probably the only pure form of surfing. Although I haven't bodysurfed naked yet, that might be the ultimate. The thing I really enjoy about bodysurfing is that not only are you surfing and getting really fit as well, but you learn to appreciate a wave so much more, and you learn how to use the power it offers you.

Mark Cunningham was a huge inspiration to me long before I met him. I'd hear about him out at Pipe by himself when no one else would go out there, a guy who charged but also just had this connection with the sea. I think there's a certain knowledge of waves that you can only get if you bodysurf. A lot of my friends are good bodysurfers. Me, Strider Wasilewski, and Keoni Watson used to bodysurf Pipeline on big days, and we'd never use fins because we wanted to feel natural. The average ten-foot day at Pipe, there are a lot of good four-foot waves that you wouldn't even notice unless you were bodysurfing.

There's this really fun thing to do when you're bodysurfing. When a really steep wave comes at you, maybe one that's a little too late to take off on, you swim right up the curve of the face underwater. The momentum of the wave pushing up the face will throw you out the back of it. I was bodysurfing at Pipe one day, and my friend Vava swam out and we got this shot.

Pipeline,
2007.

Vava
Ribeiro
(photographer)

It was just a medium day at Pipe. I'm not a water photographer. I was just cruising around with a small camera, looking for unusual images. I was sitting on the shoulder with my camera, and Kelly came out bodysurfing. He said to me, watch this. I'm going to punch through a wave and get air on the other side. I had one last shot on my Nikonos 5, so I just waited for him to punch through and shot it just at the right moment. It's a great shot of Kelly because he is an enigmatic character. It looks like he's being born of the ocean. It's just spitting him out. There's mystery and energy in it.

*****
*****
*****

We
were
on
King
Island
with
a
bunch
of friends.
I'm not sure
whether
Sean Davey,
Eddie Vedder,
or Joe Curren
actually shot
this (Eddie—Ed.),
but I grabbed
Eddie's ciggie
and took a fake
drag off it.
Kinda felt like
my late father,
but the truth is
I can't breathe
those things in.
I'll always wonder
how people can smoke.
This ran as a full page
without explanation in
an Australian surf mag!

I was down in Barbados

S
P
E
E
D

where this buddy of mine, Paul Bourne, is a rally car driver. He's a surfer, and my brother Sean and I have known him since 1985 when I was down there on a school trip. In 2001, Paul and a couple other Barbados drivers got their cars out, and we closed the circuit down and made this giant figure eight. You'd do these turns with two-hundred-yard power slides, not even holding the steering wheel, just stomping on the gas and riding it. Paul ended up hitting a boulder and wrecking his car, but it was a total blast.

I went back last year, and Paul actually let me drive his car, but he's about six-four and the car is built exactly to his specs. I had to wedge about two or three towels behind me on the seat, then really bunch them up so I could get my feet to the pedals. The gear ratios are really close together. First gear starts out low and runs pretty high, but after that the gears are really close. This car has 600-plus horsepower, costs about $250,000, and the last thing I wanted to do was wreck it! There are about six or seven turns on the course, and it runs for a kilometer or so; from anywhere on it you can pretty much see the whole course. They closed the gates, and there were about six or eight of us. Paul took us all for a ride and then he let me drive.

I went real slow the first lap and a couple times just stomped on the gas to see what would happen. The horsepower was frightening, particularly with the car stripped back to almost nothing. Each lap I got a little quicker, and one time I came around this corner a little too quick. Paul had told me to kind of slow it down on the corners, and I could see I was making him nervous, so I slowed it back down.

In 2006, I was invited to do the celebrity race at the Melbourne Grand Prix but I couldn't accept. They invited me again in 2007, and there was no way I was going to miss it. You have to do a week-long training course, but the night before I was supposed to fly down, I had a major flood in my new apartment on the Gold Coast and missed the first day's training. They let me do a couple of catch-up laps the second morning before everyone got there, gave me a little tutorial, and said good luck.

I never had fear for a second. Not that the cars were totally crazy—120 or 140 horsepower, hardly anything—but we were driving them as fast as we possibly could, going sideways around corners, trying to stay in control with twenty-seven other novices all around the track. A couple of people totaled their cars during the training week, so there were inherent dangers, but going fast seemed so natural to me.

Barbados power slide.

Friday they take us to the course at Albert Park, where we have twenty-five minutes of practice, then another twenty the next day, then the race is on. I went out there and tried to go as fast as I possibly could, thinking if F-1 cars can do 220 mph on this course, surely I can get this thing moving. I ended up going off the track five times—three times in my first lap. At the end of the day another guy and I got called up to the principal's office, the licensing authority known as CAMS. The guy calls me over and says he has reports of me going off the track on five separate occasions, so what did I have to say for myself? I said I just drove too fast, I didn't know the course. He goes, well, you can't drive like that tomorrow; this is serious business and you have to stay on the course. Wow, this was serious! So serious in fact that the other guy on report had his license pulled.

Race day comes and we're off. By the time we hit the first corner I was in second, and by the end of the first lap I was in first, and I led most of the second lap. Then I had the same problem I'd had all week. Shifting with my left hand, I kept going from second to first when I was looking for third and almost dropping the transmission out of the car. I'm red-lining in second and dropping back to first, and the car is basically going backward! I did it three times in the race, one of them on the final turn and once when I was in the lead and three cars just went straight past me. I ended up third. The whole thing was really fun, a great experience that I'd love to do again. It's not that great for the environment, but it's a blast.

With Bruce Gilbert, Barbados.

As a kid I lived behind a golf course,

GOLF

and my best friend and I used to wade through the little lakes and the creek and find balls in the mud. We'd try to hawk the balls on the course, but we got caught, so we stopped doing that. Plus there were alligators in the swamps. I tried to hit golf balls quite a few times over the years and just couldn't do it. I guess as a kid I had the idea that golf was kind of lame, not very cool, so I didn't get into it.

In 1995 a friend of mine in Florida, Mitch Varnes, invited me to play a round of golf with him while we talked about business. We never got around to talking business, and I was literally hooked from that day. I think I hit maybe one or two shots that felt right and went where I wanted them to, so I thought that was cool. But the game also seemed superchallenging, so I went back and played the next day, and that was it. Totally sucked in.

Rob Machado started to play around that same time, so we started playing together. That winter in Hawaii we played in a tournament at Turtle Bay with some other surfers. Then a bunch of us on tour started playing, and we all got hooked, so much so that John Shimooka and Ross Williams came to Florida to have a golf week with me, and we only surfed once! What sucked me in was that it was such a simple thing, and yet such a difficult thing to master. I could relate it to surfing, which I think is the same. Think about how much there is to learn between when you first stand up and when you carve your first bottom turn . . . there's a lot of learning between those two places. Surfing and golf are both about repeating simple moves in a consistent way to get the desired result.

In 1996 and '97, I played much more golf than I surfed, and I had my best two competitive years on tour. I won twelve tour events over the two years, with seven out of thirteen in '96. I attribute that to my golf! I don't know if people will understand that, but what golf did for me was to make me think about my form and my technique. I'd read Ben Hogan's *Five Lessons,* and I started to think about technique for surfing and whether those lessons could be applied—whether how you create speed and power in a golf swing could apply to the way you ride a wave. Golf also taught me more about being competitive and being ready for the unexpected. In golf you never know what's going to happen on the next hole; in surfing something amazing could happen on the next wave.

With all these ideas going through my head, I started to write them down and to develop a "Surf Lesson." In my mind it was a book called "The Surf Lesson," but it might be a lifetime process because I keep thinking of more things I want to put in there. Just the idea of how your arms and legs and hips and shoulders relate to your board and to its movement along the wave. That can lead to a very complex equation, but what it boiled down to was how to get my body into a neutral position above my board, no matter what part of the wave I was riding, and to minimize my movements so that they became as efficient as possible. After a while I began to find that I would be surfing in a contest after not surfing for a while, and I'd be constantly thinking about how my body related to my board and to the face of the wave, according to the principles I'd come up with, and thinking took the place of practice! That is basically the method I've applied to my surfing ever since, and it comes directly from golf.

I believe people are able to achieve big things when they have an open mind, and certainly time away from surfing opened my mind to other things and helped me recharge. It also helped me focus because I'd realize I'd been playing golf and not practicing. But I think the physical aspects, the biomechanics, were really important, and I felt like I'd tapped into something that no one else knew. I wouldn't say that it changed my surfing, but I would say that it gave me a deeper understanding of it.

I get to play three or four celebrity tournaments a year. I got to play with [Australian pro] Adam Scott recently. This is probably my greatest golf story. I had to fly to Maui the morning of the tournament really early because we had an eight o'clock tee time, but I slept too late and missed the flight. I didn't get to the tournament until the fifth hole, and I find I'm with Adam Scott, and Butch Harmon is walking with us. Butch is Adam's coach, and he was Tiger's coach, probably the greatest golf coach around. So I was a little in awe, and the first ball I hit I just topped it, and I think both Adam and Butch were laughing at me.

I put it together a little as the day wore on, and we get to the eighteenth hole, which is another one of the great holes in golf, a six-hundred-yard-long par five, but it's downhill. You're hitting toward Molokai, and you can see all the whales jumping in the channel. We're down the freeway and Adam is about two hundred forty yards from the green, and he hits a shot about twenty feet onto the green, putting for eagle. Butch goes, "That is a fine golf shot, maybe the shot of the day." I'm like two hundred thirty out, and I grab a five iron and hit the shot exactly the way I wanted to, everything happens perfectly, and Butch is standing about ten yards behind me. The ball lands about five feet off the green, kicks left, and rolls toward the pin. It rolls for like twenty seconds, stopping maybe five inches from the cup, almost a double eagle. Butch grabs me by the shoulders and starts yelling, "That's a fucking golf shot!" I was so stoked, the crowd at the green just erupted, and that was my twenty seconds of golf fame, right there. That night we were at a party, and Vijay Singh comes up and says, "Hey, I heard about your shot today . . ."

Swinging
on
Cocoa
Beach.

Peff Eick (golf buddy, mentor)

I'm not sure that I would have become as close a friend as I am [with Kelly] other than the fact that he started playing golf. I play golf, and we had that in common. Kelly, Ross Williams, and I were playing at Turtle Bay one day, and this was when he was starting to get really good. It seemed like he could mimic anybody. We were on maybe the sixteenth hole, and he realized that we were tied on two over par. We tied that hole and the next, and we're looking at each other like it's game on. We get to the eighteenth and both hit a good drive on a par-five hole. He hits like a two-hundred-twenty-five-foot drive up and over the water to get to the green. I lay up and get ready to hit my third shot onto the green, and I could see the competitiveness rising up in Kelly. He hits this perfect ball onto the green and birdies the hole. I par the hole, and he beats me by a stroke. I was a victim of Kelly's competitiveness, and I don't think I've come close to beating him since. That was seven or eight years ago, and he's gotten really good since then.

It seemed like he was always pretty good. He and Ross learned together. I only get over to the North Shore four or five times a year. I would see Kelly usually after Christmas, and we'd play. He was always good, which is pretty amazing. He doesn't seem to get frustrated; he seems to be in control of his emotions. I play golf with a lot of different people, and you can pretty much tell what a person is like if you play a round of golf with them. You can tell if they're going to cheat you or try to manipulate you or play games with you. With Kelly you can tell that he's intense, highly competitive, and in control.

I've given Ben Hogan's *Five Lessons* to so many people over the years, and I believe I gave it to Kelly. It's a little white book that Hogan wrote back in the 1950s, and it's got sketches and diagrams of how he swings and how he sets up his shots. It's almost the bible of golf; ask any professional. So Kelly's playing in the Pebble Beach Pro Am, and I'm looking for him while I'm watching on TV, trying to spot him. The commentator on the Golf Channel starts talking about how Kelly had mentioned to her that he had read Ben Hogan's book and that he had applied some of it to his surfing. Well, the Golf Channel picked up on this like crazy. I don't know if Kelly thought this out beforehand or whether it was spur of the moment, but this just endeared him to serious golfers. They talked about it for the next two days, kept interviewing him about it, and kept going back to this connection between golf and surfing.

this spread: Adventures with Horny, Mentawais, 1996

1

When I was a kid I used to go as fast as I could along the face and fly out the back as high as possible, but just to try and get air, not to make anything of it. This sequence is just a backside kickout where I caught the rail just right and was able to control the board. You can see me using my back foot to stabilize the board. I was too far off the back of the wave to try and land. With that much speed coming down, you need to land down the face and go straight into the transition to have any chance of making these.

2

3

4

5

6

For the road

The gypsy trail.

This is in France. Bruce Gilbert and I were at Bourdain, watching the surf, probably a day or two before flying to Ireland on our next adventure, and then that fashion shoot in Paris described in the previous chapter. The wind was howling that day, and these seagulls were trying to fly into the wind. We were tripping out watching them. These are the extremes of my life, I guess. A couple days later I was doing a photo shoot in Paris.

THE

GYPSY

TRAIL

So many times I feel

that I just don't want to move. I go through a stage before I go on a trip where I get really stressed out about everything, unless I'm excited, like I know the surf is going to be great. I try to travel as minimally as possible and just take the things that will instantly make me feel at home—favorite clothes, notebooks, computer. I have a pretty set program most places I go in the world. In France I'll stay with [Quiksilver Europe president] Pierre Agnes in his guest house, and that becomes my home for a month of the year. In Australia I have an apartment, and that becomes my base for a couple of months.

I pretty much feel comfortable wherever I go in the world, even in landlocked Eastern European countries where people don't speak a lot of English. It's good to get out of your comfort zone because that's when you learn things. On the tour, though, I want comfort, and thanks to a lot of good friends, I have it. I take a backpack for the plane, a ukulele, my check-in travel bag, and my board bag with six or seven boards. If I can get away with it, I'll take only two or three boards because a lot of places I go I'll have boards there already. The first things I pack are my journals, my computer, and my uke.

Victory plunge, a Mundaka tradition.

I was seventeen when I first came here.

Tom Curren and I both had the same sponsors at the time, Rip Curl and Op, so I stayed at Tom's house, although I didn't know him very well. He was a hero to me, and he gave me a guided tour of the whole place. I slept in a car at Mundaka, I surfed Lafitenia—I fell in love with the whole lifestyle, and actually thought about buying a house here. Tom and Marie [Curren] knew all the good places to eat, and they introduced me to people like [French photojournalist] Alain Gardinier and a lot of surfers I'm still friends with to this day. I feel totally comfortable here.

Mundaka is the best wave in Europe when everything is right. You get a good day at Hossegor, say at Graviere, it's probably more fun because there are more waves, and it's easier to be in the spot to catch them. Mundaka gets so crowded when it's really good, particularly at the time of year I'm here. Last time I surfed, there were over a hundred people in the water. Such an amazing day. I would have still been happy if there'd been two hundred people in the water, but tempers tend to flare no matter what when it's that crowded.

Stephen Bell (a.k.a. "Belly Slater") (caddy, friend)

I met him on his first trip to France when he was surfing at Estagnots with Tom Curren. I didn't really know who he was. When he came out of the water, we sat on the sand hill and watched Tom surf, just mesmerized. We hit it off straight away, and we've been friends for eighteen years. We've worked at contests together for the past six or seven years.

He's in his comfort zone in France, he's among friends, he's got his own space, he's got his golf. There are plenty of activities to keep him interested. He's nocturnal; he'll stay up all night on his computer. It's not just that he doesn't want to hang around at the contest. It's that he's from a different generation now. The French media always want to get Kelly doing stuff with Jeremy Flores, but they're from different generations! The only people Kelly's got left on tour he can relate to are Taylor Knox and the Hobgoods. That's why France is so good for him. He has this other world away from the contests.

TAVARUA (FIJI)

The first time I went there was 1990,

right after I signed with Quiksilver, and we were making *Kelly Slater in Black & White.* I was eighteen, and I'd been dreaming of going there for years, having heard all the stories about the fishing and diving and great waves. It seemed like the ultimate place when I was a kid. Then when I got there, it was a bit like going to school. My brother Sean had been there a few years before me, so the people felt they already knew me, same as my teachers did at school. A big section of *Black & White* featured Tavarua with interviews with [village head man] Big John and some of the others. It created a good connection. Plus there's just something about the place that makes you feel connected. I got close with Scott Funk, who was one of the guys running the island then, and he invited me to come back and be a boat driver. I was actually going to do that in '91, but then they started to have problems with other surfers coming by boat, and the villages were having problems between themselves over the business side of things. For a couple of years it was a bit sketchy. I went back in '93 with Brock Little, and when it was good there'd be thirty guys in the lineup. They got the problems sorted out, and I've been back every year since. I've had my own event there. [Chief] Druku told me, "You're welcome on my island any time as my guest." I just have this wonderful connection with those people. I love them, and for some reason they love me.

Tavarua
rights
hiding
from
the
sun
on
a
long
session
without
enough
sunscreen.

I'd been wanting to do an event for some time because I had these ideas about how contests should be judged and run, and I really wanted to put them into action. On the pro tour we have ten-day waiting periods. Since Tavarua gets booked week to week, there were three or four days sitting free, so we piggybacked the Kelly Slater Invitational onto the front end of the Quiksilver Pro Fiji and took advantage of the fact that the pros were coming there anyway. The idea was to test out things that would make pro surfing better, but we also invited some celebrities—and I hate to use that word—who have a passion for surfing. There was no pressure on them to perform; they were just able to relax and experience what we do. It's cliché to say but it was a very organic experience. A lot of people said it was the best trip ever. On a personal level, when I saw people like Perry Farrell from Jane's Addiction and Tony Hawk and Jackson Browne not wanting to leave, that was pretty special. For me, getting to know Jackson was memorable. I'll never forget my brother Sean and I sharing a mike and singing along with all those great songs that we'd grown up listening to.

Perfection at Cloudbreak. Nothing better.

Jamming at the KS Invitational, Kelly, Sean, and Jackson Browne.

113

When you're in that fortunate position

of being able to go somewhere that no one has ever surfed, it's pretty exciting. That was what the Crossing was all about. For six years it cruised the tropics searching for unridden waves and checking on the health of coral reefs. Probably the best memory I have of it is the first trip, when I was on the boat with my brother Stephen, Veronica Kay, and Troy Brooks. Horny [Jeff Hornbaker] and Don King were shooting it, Martin Daly was the skipper. We flew to Port Moresby to get on and steamed out toward the Solomon Islands. We had amazing fishing, but we didn't get much surf. There were all these reef passes with perfect setups. The wind was pretty calm most of the time, and if there'd been swell, it would have been amazing. I think the swell did get up a bit after I'd left, but I spent ten days on the boat and surfed maybe half a dozen waves that were chest-high.

The ocean life there was unbelievable. We were at one place getting ready to surf, and we'd heard stories that there were crocodiles around this island. We were a little freaked out, but we were on a barrier reef a ways out so we thought we'd be fine. Driving out through the channel we saw a huge pod of dolphins beneath us, then a bunch of sharks sort of below them and mixed in with them. Every time we stopped the boat, six or eight sharks would come up to investigate. We dove with them quite a bit and got used to being around them. It's much scarier to be on a surfboard if you've seen sharks in the vicinity than to be down there interacting with them where you see how they act in their natural environment.

[handwritten captain's log:] reading on the depth meter sounded from 60 feet one second to 250 the next. There's a good possibility of losing the boat out there. We've ventured into a number of villages. Their means and ways are simple. Eat what is available, build from that which already stands here. Nails are scarce. Radios don't seem to exist. They had collected a few shells from the beaches and had necklaces called EBARAGU which celebrated happiness but seemed to have no conventional form like jewelry we know, just some shells a couple beads and a few more shells on string in no particular order or shape. One old woman of 90 or so had no teeth but smiled bright as day. Plumerias covered her shy smile and seemed to make you forget her age. She seemed like a young child. Not a care in this simple, uncomplicated, never-changing world. Nothing to cloud her vision or make her sad except maybe the makeshift cemetery adjacent to her home, her open shack. She had tattoos all down her arms and she offered Jeff one. He settled for a younger lady's EBARAGU. Behind her shack was a burnt stamp amidst tall beautiful palms. A straw hat covered the stamp. I took it off to put on and take a photo as a huge, brown spider kept out and chased me away, only to hide under a giant clam shell that seemed to be hundreds of years old. That got us on to conversations of how animal and insect life ever even found their way here. For instance, beautiful red and green parrots buzzed our heads numbers of times this day as we walked the shore finding shells. How did they get here? How does anything get here? Even us? Maybe the fish lead us.

On that trip some beautiful shots came out of meeting these islander kids in their canoes. Unfortunately I had to leave the boat early and missed that experience, but my brother Stephen was there. He told me they were so excited, screaming and laughing every time he caught a wave. It was literally their first experience of surfing, even though their culture had been involved with the ocean for thousands of years. That was the beauty of the Crossing, the way it brought surfing to so many people who didn't know about it.

I wrote in the captain's log about an amazing old woman we met. *"Plumerias covered her shy smile and seemed to make you forget her age. She seemed like a young child. Not a care in this simple, uncomplicated, never-changing world."* We were in the middle of nowhere—they said maybe a dozen boats a year came through. The villagers had a chalkboard, and they were studying math. It struck me as odd because there were only a dozen people there, and you didn't expect to see them studying. Of course the missionaries had come through generations before and taught them to read and write, but it still seemed very odd out here in the middle of nowhere.

this spread:
Quiksilver
Crossing,
1999.

I'm not really sure how this came about.

[Photographer] Sean Davey was involved, and this guy, Wire, who's friends with Derek Hynd. I was off the tour at the time in '01, and I'd been in Australia for a while, surfing with Derek. [Pearl Jam's] Eddie Vedder happened to be in Sydney with his girlfriend. Eddie's kind of a quiet guy who doesn't really enjoy being on the scene, so I thought maybe he'd like to have a surf trip. I called him and he said, absolutely, let's go.

It was freezing cold, but the waves were really fun. The swells wrap around the island from both directions. They start out as west swells, then a day or two into the swell, they'll start wrapping around the east side of the island, too. You get these incredible peaks up and down the beach at a place called Martha's. We checked spots all over the island and surfed a couple that probably hadn't been surfed before—real gnarly, sharky feeling spots by the lighthouse. We also surfed this mushy left point break. Eddie had never ridden a shortboard, and Derek had brought down a couple of boards that were quite buoyant, copies of Occy's okd board from '84, so we paddled him out to the point and got him up on one. He really dug it.

The second night we were there we had this huge bonfire. A friend of mine named Red Whyte from Bells Beach who surfs and plays music was with us, and we jammed on this song of his called "The Lucky Country." We all started playing by the fire, and I guess word got around and people started showing up. There were about fifty people there, probably the biggest party ever on King Island. For some reason there were tons of wild turkeys running around everywhere, and we got the idea to catch one to eat, but they were too fast and they'd go up the trees. So there we are drinking Wild Turkey, throwing rocks at wild turkeys. Some kids eventually hit one out of a tree with rocks and killed it but I'm not sure it was ever eaten. Strange night.

The next day the swell seemed to have dropped, so we took our time driving out to Martha's and checked out a few places along the way. At one point there's a hill where some local spells out words using old tires, and this day the tires spelled out, "Kelly . . . who is she?" I guess they were talking about me. When we got there, it was four or five feet and peeling down the beach, just perfect spitting barrels. It was a rare east swell. Wire had really become friendly with Eddie, and it turned out he'd had two heart attacks. He told Eddie that when he woke up in the hospital after his second attack, he was singing Pearl Jam's "Alive." Needless to say, Eddie was very moved.

opposite: With Eddie Vedder enjoying downtime and a huge bonfire in King Island, Australia, 2001

King Island, Australia, 2001.

The first time I ever heard anything about the place

JEFFREYS BAY

was when Occy won there in 1984. What I heard was that it's a place that really tests you as a surfer, really highlights your strengths and weaknesses. It's about speed and flow and connecting the dots all the way down the line. Like Pipeline, I guess, it was a wave that I really wanted to succeed at riding. Whenever I saw pictures of it, I'd imagine the lines I would have drawn on it. One thing I noticed was that very few people turned right back into the whitewater. There was a lot of down-the-line stuff, hitting the lip, lots of floaters, basically letting the wave do the work. I wanted to take it on. It is one of the classic waves of the world, and I wanted to test myself on it.

J-Bay definitely exists in a surf bubble. If you just go there and surf, eat, and go to bed, you don't really notice the township five minutes away up the backside of the point and the tremendous amount of poverty there is, like in so much of Africa. The town is built on surfing and fishing, and a lot of people do both.

As a young surfer I had this dream that if I was successful, I'd own a house at all of the great point waves of the world. About five years ago I came very close to buying a house at Jeffreys. It was a house owned by ['60s surfer] Mike Tabeling, who was moving back to Florida. During that period I got connected with the local surf school. I was eating dinner a lot at Kitchen Windows, where the surf club operates from. I got to know all the kids, and they became my informal caddies. Between heats we'd be wrestling and messing around and having fun. I gave them some boards and a little money to help keep their school going. One kid I got very close to, really took a shine to him. When I went back the next year I asked after him and was told that he'd started sniffing glue, which a lot of them do.

I never went to the old South Africa, pre-Mandela. I first came in '92, right around the time when Mandela got out of jail and things started to change. But with the AIDS epidemic, unemployment, and poverty, it's still hard for a lot of people. It seems like race clashes have become less frequent, and I can tell you that I feel comfortable there. I don't feel unsafe. What a wonderful thing for Mandela to come back and lead his country. I recently got this text from a friend who was in South Africa:

"Dude, we just had lunch with Nelson Mandela which was fucking amazing. We started talking about surfing and your name came up and Nelson said, 'That man Kelly Slater, my grandson follows him, he is a very focused man . . .' How fucking cool is that!"

Pretty damn cool. I've saved that for *my* grandchildren!

I'd been wanting to go to Ireland for years.

I R E L A N D

Enjoying the craic in Bundoran.

left:
From left to right, Gabe Davies, Briohny Radda, Richie Fitzgerald, unidentified woman, KS, and Andy Keegan.

I don't know enough about my heritage to know where we're from, but I believe the Slaters were from the South. Anyway, my friends Gabe and Lauren Davies were going over, and he called me when he got there and said he'd just got the best waves of his life. He was laughing like a little kid. My friend, Bruce Gilbert, and I still had a little window before we had to fly back to the States, so we jumped on a flight and then drove from Dublin over to Bundoran. First night we went straight to Brennan's Pub and had a Guinness. They showed us this little cubicle off the front and explained that that was for the women who wanted to come in and have a drink, because pubs were for men. I'm not too big on alcohol, but it was interesting to see how big a part it played in their culture.

The next day the waves were pretty small, but we drove down to Easkey where there's this cool castle. People must have been really small back then, because it was like a collection of little cubby holes. Below the castle there are at least a dozen reefs, and as the tide came up, we surfed a little left. I was kind of hoping to be left to myself in Ireland, but Gabe had a film crew making a surf movie along with him. Everywhere we went to surf, the locals got tipped off and came out to surf with us. But the people were kind and sweet and genuine.

Leaving Ireland was quite a saga. I was trying to get out of this TV interview I had to do in Paris because I wanted to stay in Ireland a little longer. I woke up the morning of the interview, checked on flights, and rang Quiksilver and told them it just wasn't possible for me to get there. They said, we'll make it happen. Kate Winslet was the other guest and they said it was very important for Quik's relation with the TV station. So they got us a helicopter to get back to Dublin, and Gabe and Lauren, who'd never been in a helicopter, came along for the ride. In Dublin they had a private plane waiting to fly us to Paris, where it was raining like crazy, and we stepped straight into another helicopter—which flew us into the city, where we jumped in a limo for five minutes, straight to the studio and to the interview.

All things considered, it's the best place on the planet.

The French have the lifestyle, but the Tahitians have the lifestyle and the most beautiful environment you could hope to experience. The thing about Tahitians is they won't just welcome you into their house, they'll give you their house! I was there with Strider Wasilewski and Bruce Gilbert, and Raimana Van Bastolaer and his wife and daughter gave us their bedrooms. They slept on futons in front of the TV. I was jet-lagged and out of synch, so I didn't get up until really late most days, but I still managed to get into some stand-up paddling and a few waves. Tahiti has a special place in my heart, as it does with most surfers who go there. It's about the most beautiful setting you could have, with the mountains and valleys and everything so green and lush. There's not a day goes by you don't see rainbows, the water's the perfect temperature, and everyone's got a smile on their faces.

Tahiti, 2006

On a crowded day at Mundaka the average guy is going to get dropped in on or a pro is going to snake him every wave. That particular day I talked to people out there for more than an hour who hadn't had a wave, so it can be very frustrating. But if you do get that wave . . . I got a few good ones that day but this one really stood out. I'm paddling in and there's about six people waiting to drop in on me . . . they're waiting for you to catch a rail. But that wave I probably had 15 seconds of tube time. I got a long barrel, came out and then got an even longer barrel down inside where it bends. Mundaka can be absolutely mesmerizing. You get in the barrel there and you feel like you're standing under a waterfall because it just doesn't change.

6

For the show

Lights,
camera,
action!

KS
faces
down
the
surfarazzi.
ASP
banquet,
Gold
Coast,
February
'07.

Some of my earliest childhood memories are of my dad playing guitar and my mom playing banjo, but oddly enough I don't really remember them playing together much. I think both of them had dreams of singing and playing professionally at some point. My mom definitely had a good voice. I only have vague recollections of my dad singing. He never really belted it out, but he knew some Van Morrison tunes, a bit of Cat Stevens, stuff like that—Jackson Browne, John Denver. He played classic acoustic guitar and Mom had this 1939 Gibson gold top banjo, a pretty amazing instrument. Music was a huge part of our daily lives, but none of us kids played. We had a drum kit that we banged around on, but we never learned to play a beat.

Actually, I got the scar on my nose from a cymbal being thrown up in the air. Whether I threw it or my brother, I don't really know, but from that point on the music was in me, so to speak. When I was about five, apparently I used to sing a lot. One day my mom and I were being driven to the beach by my uncle Big Bob, who was my hero. I stood up in the back seat and started singing Melissa Manchester's "Midnight Blue," and I sang it from start to finish. My mom said she looked over at Big Bob, and he was crying. In fact every time she tells that story she starts to cry. I forget the song now, but back then I'd memorized it.

I didn't pick up a guitar until right before my high school graduation. My mom bought me an acoustic steel string Sigma, and I started playing. The next couple of winters was when Rob [Machado] and I would stay together on the North Shore, and [surfer and musician] Peter King would come over and teach us stuff. Jack [Johnson] was around, along with Donovan Frankenreiter and Tom Curren. On the fringe was Timmy Curran. He was a little younger, but he was very influenced by Jack. We'd put headphones on Tom and play a song that we liked, and he'd figure out how to play it immediately. We'd all be mesmerized. I found that really moving, that he could just pick it up like that, because I knew nothing formal about music and didn't realize it could be that easy to play any song. I started to teach myself to read music, but just as I was starting to understand it, I realized you could just read the chords/tabs. So I took the short cut.

I think you get that sort of thing happening in sport, in art, fashion, science, where people get together who have similar ideas and develop a path, but it's not that common for sport and music to form a liaison, except maybe basketball and hip-hop. Surfing seems to go well with the guitar and ukulele, acoustic music. I think that comes from the fact that the culture began with people camping out at the beach and strumming guitars. That definitely became a part of our lives. It sounds clichéd but it's exactly what we would do. We'd have a fire on the beach and hand a couple of guitars around and play songs we all knew. When you do that enough, the chords and the melody structure just becomes a part of you. Makes it a lot easier to learn.

You know, Jack started out playing punk music. Well, originally acoustic, of course, but his first band was punk. It was just his friends from high school. The band was called Limber Chicken. He started to tone it down at college, and I guess he got more comfortable with mellow music. I never got into the punk thing, but Rob kind of did with a band called Sack Lunch, and the Great Outdoorsmen before that. When we were learning to play, we'd drive around in Rob's car listening to the Great Outdoorsmen, songs about the neighborhood bum . . . whatever. It was pretty funny. PK [Peter King] had a few bands, but the main one was Dakota Motor Company. They made a few albums, and I sang with them a couple times early on.

GO CAT GO!

Lyrics by Ozzie Wright.

we're all irie MAN
we whites aND AFRICAN
getting ON LiFe we all caN
HANG out At THE BEACH
SPREADeN Love AND PeACE
LEARNEN FROM OUR FELLOW MA
so come ON BRiNG it DO
to BATHSHEEBA town
coconuts AND SAND

Peff Eick (friend, mentor)

I've been playing the guitar since I was seventeen, so years ago we'd have barbecues at the Johnson house next door to me on the North Shore, and I'd pull out my guitar and play long before any of the kids played music. They enjoyed it, and eventually they took to it. Jack took to it very quickly, Kelly took a little longer. He'd learn a riff, and I'd lecture him, "Kelly, you have to learn a song from beginning to end." A lot of people learn the hook but never the song. Now I think Kelly is getting really good. His songwriting has come on, and I think he has great potential.

With the Beautiful Girls, Duranbah, '07.

Jack Johnson (musician, surfer, friend)

We built guitars one time for a couple of weeks in my dad's shed, just working away all hours of the night. We stayed up late working on them the night before he won one of his world titles at the Pipe Masters. I remember saying, Hey, we should go to bed, and Kelly was like, "Ah, I can't sleep right now." We stayed up until after two in the morning, sanding and mixing sawdust with glue to put in the cracks. I was so scared that he was going to lose a world title and it'd be my fault!

Pamela Anderson (actress, friend)

We'd hang out on the North Shore in the house next to Jack Johnson. It's crazy, you know, all these songs I'm hearing on the radio, I remember Jack and Kelly singin' 'em around the campfire. Kelly would go missing for a few hours, and no one knew where he was. Then he'd come back, and he's been off whittling a guitar out of a tree!

One time we played a gig

at the Sunset Elementary School. It was Donovan, Jack, me, PK, and Rob, and Curren played drums. I sang, Jack played bass. It was a pretty full on surf band. Donovan was trying to do lead, but he didn't really know how yet. We played three songs we'd written, sitting around at Jack's house. I don't think there were that many big gigs on the North Shore back then, probably around '95. I think [surfboard shaper] Pat Rawson's band may have played after us. Rob, Peter, and I all wore the same Ke Nui brand shirts, Pete Johnson's company. That was our Beach Boys getup or something. I think I still have my shirt.

Around this time a guy named Roger "Snake" Klein, who worked for Epic Records, had been hanging out with PK in Orlando, working on an MTV show called *Sandblast*. One day they came over to Cocoa Beach to go surfing. They were hanging out at my house, and PK told him we'd written a couple of songs, so we played them for him. Roger goes, "We should record this stuff. In fact, why don't we do an album?" I didn't really know who the guy was or what he did, but within a year it had become a reality. He was the one who put us together with T-Bone Burnett. I liked some of the bands that T-Bone had produced, and Roger arranged a meeting with him at T-Bone's house in L.A. We sang him our songs, and he just closed his eyes, then wrote down a few notes and critiqued my singing and the song structure a bit. Then he said, "Okay, I'll work with you guys."

That was what he said. I'm not sure what he really thought! We tossed around a few names for the band, but every time we'd show up to record it was like, "Oh, here come the surfers." So we became the Surfers.

I was in awe of T-Bone. One of the first times I went to his house, Elvis Costello was there. I suddenly realized, Whoa, we're in the thick of the music world here. Suddenly we were professional musicians by default. I wasn't prepared for it at all, and it scared me a bit. I felt unworthy. I had a hard time processing the fact that we were in with an album coming out on a major label.

top left: Music with Moby as a guest on the radio show I used to do with Sirius Radio. One of the many interesting musical connections I've had in my life.

right: Rockin' at the Sunset Elementary.

Pamela Anderson

I don't really think Kelly wanted to be on the *Baywatch* set. He didn't really fit. But you know, I think Kelly has that same presence everywhere he goes. He's there, but he's not. He lives in his own world, does his own thing. When you get him, you get him. On *Baywatch*, they were always looking for him. He'd have gone off surfing. He wasn't a natural actor, but I don't think anybody was on that show. *Baywatch* was not about acting. It was absolutely huge in 150 countries because you can watch it with the sound off.

When I appeared on the *Baywatch* television series in the early '90s, I never felt like I belonged in that world. I was there in body but not in spirit. This was different because it was based on something I had a real passion for. But there was an element of unreality, too. I felt like I should have made a few albums by myself and worked my way up to this. But PK had made a few albums and worked on others, so he brought a level of comfort for the rest of us. He was really the leader, but there was this focus on me being the singer that I didn't really enjoy. I wanted to sing and write and make music, and there are parts of the album that really mean a lot to me. We wrote a song about Todd Chesser called "Not Your Slave." I remember PK and I sitting in the studio crying as we wrote the lyrics. It was only six months after he'd drowned, so it was very raw, and I guess that helped us put a little closure to Todd's passing.

Strangely for someone who'd spent a lot of years on the pro surfing tour, I found touring with the band really difficult. You play, you stay up late, then the next day, you have to travel again. I hated it, actually—which is not to say I didn't have fun. The guys were a blast, and we had some memorable experiences. One night we played in Fort Lauderdale to maybe thirty people. There were more of us than them! There was a hurricane coming and everyone was being evacuated. We played to this little group, and it was such fun, like we were playing in our backyard. A lot of the people were our friends anyway, and it turned into a celebration.

The Surfers toured in the USA, Germany, and Japan, where we made our farewell tour in 2000. We opened for Pearl Jam in Florida on a sidestage in front of 18,000 people and sold around 70,000 copies of our album, *Songs from the Pipe,* so while we didn't set the world on fire, we did okay. Maybe we sold 60,000 of them in Japan. I'm not quite sure.

I think I like the idea of just writing by myself and recording in my spare time while I'm traveling. Back then, there was no way I could have done an album without Peter and Rob. One of our songs, "Never," was used on the soundtrack of the movie *In God's Hands.* I wrote the lyrics to that on a plane going to Australia. When I got back, Peter wanted to put down a vocal track for it, and he asked if I had any lyrics. I said I'd written some but didn't like them and threw them away. He goes, Well, where did you throw them? He made me go and fish them out of a trash can. I sang them and ended up really loving the lyric. For some reason I didn't want to sing them but I was glad Peter pulled them out of the trash.

"Never" was about people I knew who were always going to give up drugs or drinking, then the next time you see them, it's the same old shit again. To me this song kind of symbolized that mentality.

I think anyone who's ever written a song will tell you they can come from anywhere. Sometimes you'll start playing a chord, and the words just fit and the whole thing comes together. Sometimes you'll have a melody in your head, and you have to figure out the chords that go with it. Probably the best songs are the simple ones. I consider myself an amateur songwriter, but even at the high end of the game, I doubt that the process is much different. The one common thing I've found among songwriters is that their best work doesn't come from sitting down with the intention of writing a song—it just seems to come out.

left: Working on the set list with Eddie.

below: With Eddie at the Eddie.

Back in 2005 when I won my seventh world title,

Eddie Vedder wanted to celebrate with me and do a gig of some sort, maybe a stripped down acoustic set. We were going to try to organize it to coincide with Pearl Jam's tour of Australia. I'm pretty good long-term friends with [surfers and Bra Boys producers] Koby and Sunny Abberton. I surfed in the Snickers Open contest in Maroubra a couple years back, and I got interested in what was going on with the community there, so I started talking to the guys there about maybe doing a Pearl Jam benefit concert at Maroubra. That was my idea for my birthday in 2006, but Pearl Jam's tour dates changed and it never happened. Eddie always wanted to do a concert on the North Shore in support of the environmental causes that he and the whole band have been involved in for years. They've donated tens of thousands to Surfrider Foundation, for example, specifically for the Save Trestles campaign. When I won my eighth title at the end of 2006, Pearl Jam was ending its two-year world tour in Hawaii in December, playing with U2, and finally it all came together.

There was a bunch of land behind Pipeline under threat, and its defense had become known as the Pupukea Paumalu Project. A Japanese development company had owned the land for twenty years, and Jack Johnson was touring in Japan and was able to convince the management of this company to sell the land back to the people at the price they paid for it. But the money still had to be found, and so this concert became a fundraiser for the Paumalu Project.

Quiksilver got involved, and we were able to organize a concert in Waimea Valley right after the Eddie opening ceremony. Pearl Jam played for about three hundred people.

About six years earlier, Eddie had invited me on stage to play in Brisbane, and I pussed out . . . too scared of the crowd. This was my second-chance night, and I got up and played one of my favorite Pearl Jam songs, "Indifference," trading verses with Eddie, and then a Neil Young song, "Rockin' the Free World," at the end. When I went back on stage for the last song, the guitar techie ran off with the guitar, and I'm like, I thought I was gonna play guitar on this one! Then he runs back on with a different guitar for me, and it had the SL8R logo on it. I thought, this is really cool—Eddie's put the sticker on for me. Then halfway through the song, I'm looking at the guitar and I realize it's not a sticker: the guitar has been made with a plate that had that on! I was blown away. Eddie once told me Pete Townshend was his favorite because he was the first guitarist to get air. I think I was doing my impression of him by the end of the song!

It was an unbelievable gig. When we're done, I go to give the tech the guitar back, and he says, "Wait, I'll get a case for it." I went, what are you talking about? And he goes, "It's yours, man." The guitar was a gift from Gibson and Quiksilver. That's definitely one of the best gifts I could ever get.

I think when you get pretty good at doing something, you can either sit back on your laurels, and if you find that's fulfilling, then why not? But if you look at a picture like this and think that you could have been just a little deeper, just a little more vertical off the top, that's going to push your physical ability even further and open your mind to the biomechanics of what you're doing. Philosophically, I think you can learn a lot about yourself and about what's possible in the world by just taking it a little farther.

left:
Rockin' the free world with Pearl Jam, Waimea Valley, December 2006.

right:
Backstage, San Diego, 2006.

Shot 8 was used for an ad after I won my seventh title. By then you can see how gnarly the wave was, but when I took off, well, when you look at shot 3, it looks like about a six foot wave, but then it really started to mutate into an eight foot wave. It's one of those waves with a bit of north swell in it and you're almost taking off at Pipeline, and then the west wedge comes into it. There's so much energy. If you look at around shot 12, if that lip was landing on you, you'd probably end up in hospital. I remember paddling for this wave because I was so focused. I knew how intense it was going to get as I took off. I think that's Braden Dias right behind me in shot 1. There were two other guys scratching for it and Braden was one, but I was deeper and in the right spot. I remember thinking I could have been a little deeper, but if I had been, I guess I wouldn't have been as casual. As I came out I was thinking, well, I could have made it a little more difficult. Then again, in that place and in that situation it's better to err on the side of caution.

For the future

The
world
according
to
KS.

The
world-
view
from
Cocoa
Beach.

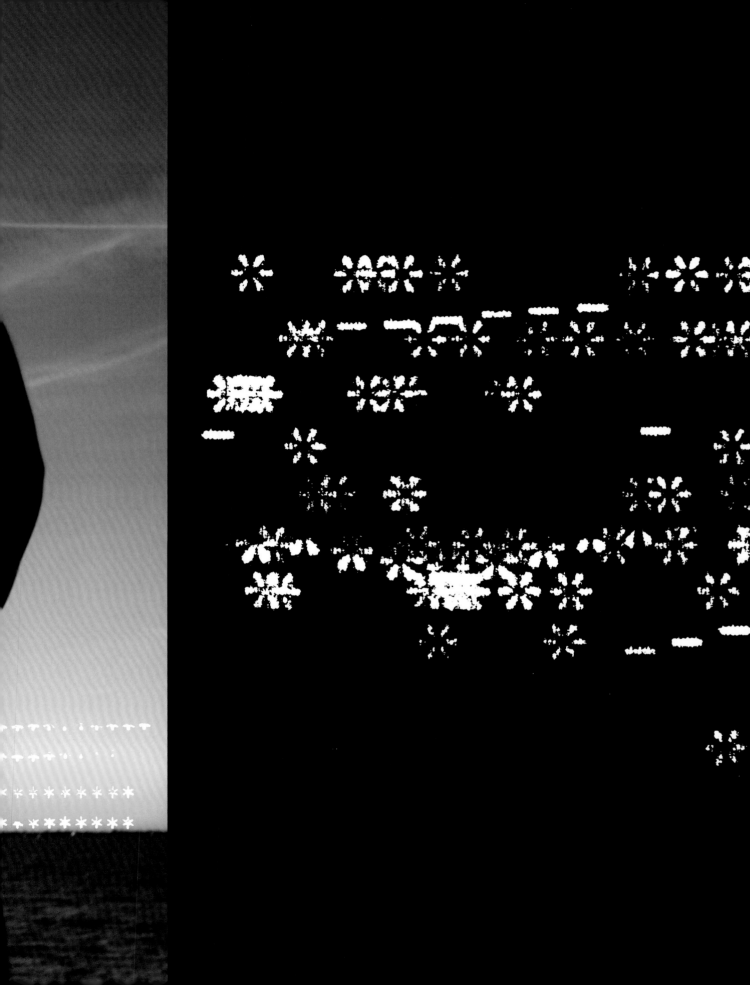

I was originally going to write a big, long view of what I think about the war we find ourselves in and the tragedies that have gotten us there and the way I see things panning out as a direct result of that. I have many opinions that aren't the most popular with those who support what has happened in the past seven years. Most Americans see it as defending America, and there's nothing anyone can say to convince them otherwise after having seen what happened in NYC on 9/11. But I think the bigger question is what was it that led us to that place and what were the reasons behind why it happened?

It seems that we have our hands in so many things around the world, apparently policing the rest of the world from the safety of our protected world in America. The only way I think we can try to see things differently is to relate what's happening to our own lives. I remember what I felt that morning watching (on TV) the planes hit the buildings. I remember feeling empty, terrified. I was having dreams, nightmares, of being on one of the planes that hit the towers and in slow motion watching the view from inside the planes as they smashed headlong into the side of the building, crumbling and exploding with fire as people were smashed into nothing and the buildings were enveloped in a ball of flames. I woke up in a ball of sweat for about a week afterward.

As we were told, that's what the terrorists wanted us to feel. I immediately thought, "fucking Bin Laden" like everyone else probably did. That event led me on a search to find out what really might've happened, not only there and in Washington but in the years leading up to that fateful day. Instead of telling everyone what my exact feelings and beliefs are about the situation and either preaching to the choir or turning people off, I would just ask this: what if you were to wake up and go to sleep every day of your life and feel that way all the time?

The net effect of what is happening in the Middle East is nothing short of a human tragedy that's been ongoing since the first Gulf War in 1990, when I was eighteen years old. Bombing has not ceased since that day. The infrastructure of the country is beyond repair and children are dying in record numbers of cancers, starvation, and malnutrition as water, food, land, and air is polluted as the result of the war we've waged in retaliation to 9/11. I don't know about you, but I have yet to see the evidence that says we should've gone there and done what we've done. I still don't see the connection that these countries had to attacking us, as it was supposedly nineteen guys from mostly Saudi Arabia, our big ally in that part of the world.

I do see a huge problem with oil and the future of energy dependence happening all over the world. I would find it hard to believe that our country didn't see this coming long before the public felt it. So now we find ourselves in a new era of fear and worry in the world, and the truth is that's what happens when people don't care about each other and take the time to know how it is for someone else and how you can truly help. I'm not saying there aren't crazy people out there beyond help, hell-bent on killing others, because that's obvious. And you can't fix everyone's problems, but I think this is a personal wake-up for us all to just take the time to talk and listen to each other more and take inventory of the lives we lead.

One interesting thing I've noticed in our recent (2008) presidential debating is that suddenly it's real popular to say that you were against the war from the beginning, especially if you are a Democrat. I also find it interesting that most of the people saying that were not vocalizing it when it came time to vote their conscience in the events after 9/11. There was only one congresswoman I remember standing up and saying much of anything and that was Cynthia McKinney. She lost her next election because of her questioning of the war and our president, but was re-elected two years later as public opinion of the war began to shift. It takes a lot of guts to speak out against not only popular opinion but also the powers that be who you essentially work for.

But for me, here's what it really all boils down to: If when you do something your intention is to help people, you're going to get something positive from it. If your intention is to get something for yourself, especially at the risk of hurting other people, then something bad will likely come your way.

Pipe.

I
R
A
Q

B
O
A
R
D

This is my political statement board.

While I think what our country is doing is wrong, the fact is, if the terrorists would put their guns down, we wouldn't shoot them. There are two sides to this. When I see or hear of a family in Baghdad sitting in their house and a bomb blows the shit out of their lives, and we did it . . . I feel some sort of responsibility. Bruce Gilbert's friend did this poster based on the iPod ads, but with pictures of a soldier with a grenade launcher and a guy being shocked in Abu Ghraib prison, and so on. It's a light-hearted take on a serious situation. The original poster had the number of Iraqis killed and the number of American troops killed, and that number has jumped dramatically since the poster was done. Noam Chomsky says if you look at the war in black-and-white terms, you've got as many American troops dead in Iraq now as Americans who died in 9/11, actually more, not to mention more than a million Iraqis and others. This board is my statement. Some people are stoked, some people are offended. I just tell them these are my favorite war images. I rode this board in the Chile WCT event last year. At that point, I guess it became a statement.

Iraq board, 2006.

When I think about the environment,

I immediately think of the amount of garbage we create. A guy named Chris Jordan created an art exhibition about that called "Running the Numbers." He's taken examples of our startling mass consumption— like the fact that in America we use 2,000,000 plastic beverage bottles every five minutes—and he illustrates it by using the actual objects in photographs. For example, 170,000 disposable batteries equals just fifteen minutes of battery production; 426,000 cell phones are retired in the United States every day. What do we do with all this stuff? Where does it go? More than 60,000 plastic bags are used in the United States every five seconds! Over 106,000 aluminium cans every thirty seconds. Our consumption is extraordinary.

It really bothers me. I'm a consumer, and I don't know what to do. Where do you start? In a perfect world we'd all have our own clean water supply and eat organic food, and our kids wouldn't be getting sick from sugar consumption and soy allergies and a million other things. I look at how much garbage I produce, and I'm probably not much different than the average person, so that concerns me.

I did a fast last year and that helped cut down on a week's worth of food and garbage. While I was fasting I was reading all about the process and trying to understand what I could do about my personal consumption. Let's say for one week everyone in America had to keep all the garbage they created in their kitchen—that would help concentrate your mind on looking for a resolution. What if all the garbage trucks went on strike for a week, what would happen? It would be horrible, but it would make us all work together toward a solution.

Cans Seurat, 2007 (and detail above) Depicts 106,000 aluminum cans, the number used in the United States every 30 seconds. From *Running the Numbers* by Chris Jordan.

I use more surfboards than just about anybody on the planet,

and it troubles me on a daily basis. I've been working with Channel Islands Surfboards and Biofoam blanks to move toward recyclable foam and soy-based resins, but what I've been finding is that everything you look into opens up a can of worms you have to deal with. I took a course in metaphysics, and one of the things I learned was that every time you learn 100 percent of something, you open up another 90 percent of things you need to know. The onion never peels totally. I have a friend in California who has gas stations, and he's doing biodiesel from used cooking oil, which is a great idea, but cooking oil is not going to run everybody's car because there's simply not enough. Now we're having to create it from soy and corn and whatever, so that it's competing with food sources. That's a major problem. It's said that if you used all the corn produced in America just for the purpose of fuel, it would only be about 15 percent of our needs and we produce 40 percent of the corn in the world! I recently watched a documentary called *The Future of Food*, which was about genetic modification, and how prevalent GM foods have become in our society and how little we know about the long-term effects. And, of course, a lot of soy and corn being produced now is GM, so while you think you're doing a good thing by running your car on biodiesel, it might turn out you're supporting genetic modification. Maybe biofuels should be graded on their origins, so that 1 is the worst you can get and 5 would be fuel from locally grown, organic materials.

Then there's the nuclear option. There are so many views on nuclear energy. They say it's the cheapest. And, forgetting about Three-Mile Island and Chernobyl, it's a pretty safe industry, but you end up with this toxic waste with a half-life of what, ten thousand, a hundred thousand years? Where are you going to put that? Maybe we're doomed already, but why create radioactive waste when there are other ways. We have sun and wind power, tidal and wave energy, and there is a way to tap the hydrogen in water. From what I hear, fuel from algae and then eventually cold nuclear fusion are the most hopeful, real options for the future of fuel. Anyway, we're going to run out of oil, and we have to find alternate fuels that don't totally ruin the earth.

One of the problems we have is that the capitalist system runs way behind available technology. Any photographer will tell you that. The technology exists, but you have to wait until it filters out into the market as the stuff already created gets used. Most industries work that way, and it slows the process of change. Which brings us back to the surfboard industry.

I think we're on the right track [toward sustainability], and there are people with their hearts in the right place. But usually the people whose hearts are in the right place don't have the money, and the people with the money don't want to lose it. There are enough people working on alternatives now to start making some headway. Channel Islands is the biggest surfboard manufacturer in the

Belly
adjusts
the
cap
for
a
magazine
shoot,
Capbreton,
2006.

world, but it only has 1 percent of the industry. However, if CI stumbled onto the new technology that's going to change everything; the impact would go much farther than that 1 percent. It's about industry leaders showing the way, but you're only going to be the industry leader by making the best surfboards, and right now the best surfboards are not made from environmentally friendly stuff.

That's the current reality, and to be honest we're at least ten years away from real change. I'd like to think less, but I rode a [new technology] board the other day, and in one surf I'd thrashed it completely, cracked it in three spots. It was made of more environmentally friendly foam, resin, and cloth. It was a start. I'd be really proud to have a board I could say was not going to hurt anything if I left it out in the ocean or threw it in the trash. Maybe we were onto something when we were just making boards out of wood.

I recently joined a carbon offset fund to offset all the flying I do, but even as I do that, I'm wondering if we aren't just witnessing a much broader process where the earth gets warmer and then gets colder. Thirty years ago we were told that we were at the dawn of an ice age. Who makes these calls? I think everyone wants to be the one who told you so. It's better to be safe than sorry, but I hate to be too fatalistic. In some good news . . . I just heard that the earth was almost half a degree warmer last year than the year before, so I guess that's good or bad news depending on who you're talking to. I mean, if you're using the warming earth to make a push to change our processes and ways of doing things then it's bad news, 'cause now you need another fact to back you up, but if that means we aren't doing quite the damage to the environment, I guess it's good news. At the end of the day it shouldn't stop us from looking at the impact we're having.

At this point, I'm not sure which is worse, the trash that's filling our world's oceans and landfills, or the stuff in the air that we're forced to breathe in, but it's safe to say we've created a huge problem for ourselves. As things are changing and it's becoming more "in style" to have less impact from industries, and people are getting more and more conscious of the end result, the natural evolution seems to be going in the right direction but we definitely need to make huge changes to get from where we are today to where we need to be.

DIET

My ultimate dream

is to live on my acreage in Hawaii and grow my own food, catch my own water, and live completely free of the grid on solar and wind energy. I'd love to eventually have a Koa forest, too.

This is typical of what I eat when I'm on the road: I have some dried fruit, bananas, dates mostly. Then apples and pears. I look for fresh fruit and veggies at the local markets, stuff that I like, like avocados. I have my Superfoods Plus (or some other type of greens) supplement, which has barley, maize, chickpea, oats, linseed, mung beans, barley grass, rice. It's basically got everything you need to recover and get your body alkalized.

Do you ever think about why you're eating? Is it for pleasure? I think most of us eat for pleasure a lot of the time. When you go out to dinner, you'll go for what tastes best, not necessarily what is best for you. Ultimately the only reason you need to eat is for energy. It takes a lot of personal discipline to approach food that way, and a lot of planning. I like to wake up and have hot tea with lemon and maple syrup because at night your digestive process is doing a lot of stuff, and it's nice to flush your body with hot water. It helps to get things moving along. I don't drink coffee, except maybe sometimes in winter in Hawaii if I'm staying with Shane Dorian. I love Kona coffee, the chocolate macadamia blend. If you smell it, you have to have it. But I have my share of crap food, too, of course.

As I write this [October '07], I'm on tour in France, and here this is how my diet works: I get up and have a cup of tea, and greens with juice, then a bowl of granola with almonds in it. I don't drink milk, so I'll have some kind of milk

substitute, like almond milk. It's a total scam that you need dairy foods for calcium, but more about that in a minute. You get more from green, leafy vegetables. I might have a yogurt now and then—I love vanilla yogurt in France. Later in the day I might start on snacks, like cashews, chips, dried bananas, tuna, mustard and avocado on rice cakes. Rice cakes are boring, but I like the texture. There's nothing better to eat in the world than an avocado. If I thought I could get away with it, I'd eat chips and guacamole all day long—sometimes I do. I make my own guac mostly. For dinner my favorite thing is fish and vegetables, and a good salad, but here in France I've been eating a lot of calamari, too, with tons of garlic. I eat a little bit of red meat, no pork except a little bit of ham in France, 'cause you can't find much else to eat oftentimes when you're looking for a sandwich. Boars will eat anything, so it's often a dirty meat. I eat quite a bit of chicken, a little turkey. I like to eat a big salad with no tomatoes. I have a total aversion to tomatoes. Oh, and I love coconut juice, but as per the food combining diet that I try to follow, you don't eat fruits and veggies together, so that's usually in the mornings in a smoothie or on its own.

As for milk, way back in the 1930s a doctor named Francis Pottenger started a ten-year study on the effects of pasteurized and raw milk on nine hundred cats. One group was fed nothing but raw whole milk, while the other group had nothing but pasteurized whole milk from the same source. The raw milk group thrived, but the pasteurized milk group became listless, confused, and highly vulnerable to a number of degenerative ailments we'd normally associate with humans, like heart disease, kidney failure, thyroid dysfunction, and brittle bones.

This was startling enough, but what really caught the doctor's attention was what happened to the second- and third-generation cats. The offspring of the pasteurized group were all born with poor teeth and weak bones, a sure sign of calcium deficiency, which indicated a lack of calcium absorption from the milk. The raw milk offspring were as healthy as their parents. The third-generation produced even worse results in the pasteurized group, with many stillborn and the rest born sterile, so that ended the experiment!

At the time this research was conducted, pasteurized milk was a recent introduction; it helped the dairy industry enormously by extending the shelf life of milk. But the new milk didn't seem to do much for extending the life of the consumer. Up to this point humans had thrived on raw milk. Today it is illegal to sell raw milk in many parts of the world, including most American states, and if you can believe it, I came upon this while reading about raw milk . . . "while possession of raw milk is legal, selling it is a crime. It's also a violation of federal law to transport raw milk across state lines with the intent to sell it for human consumption. It can only be sold as pet food!" We now have a third-generation of humans taking part in the big pasteurized milk experiment, and just like Dr. Pottenger's cats, we are not looking good. Infertility and calcium deficiency are major and growing problems.

I gleaned the above information from Daniel Reid, whose books on Tao I highly recommend. His conclusion was that it is "sheer folly" to stuff kids full of pasteurized milk in order to make then grow "strong and healthy," when they simply cannot assimilate the nutrients. In fact, we should eliminate all pasteurized dairy products from their diet.

I sometimes get ribbed by my friends

for being a conspiracy theorist. I am naturally skeptical about much of the information we are fed in mainstream news and I think that much of the time we are flat out being lied to via the mass media. There are a lot of interesting ways to view the world and what's going on in it, from chemtrails to the supposedly faked lunar landing footage to the dangers of vaccinations for children and the link to autism to government complicity in drug dealings to the idea that we're fighting in Iraq for something other than oil. I'm not saying I buy into all of the conspiracy theories out there, but the truth of some things is much more interesting than what you actually hear. Think about how people tell little white lies to your face about things you know are different than they're telling you and there's really nothing at stake other than saving face or being right. Now imagine that there is a lot at stake financially, safety-wise, or otherwise, and imagine all the covering up that can be done in those circumstances. I'm not saying all these things are true or false, but they are interesting possibilities most of the time.

I watched the events of September 11 on TV as they happened, and I don't believe everything the media tells you. I'm not going to elaborate too much and of course I'm not debating that it happened, just that what we've been told is not correct. The biggest crime scene in the world was immediately taken away by trucks, never to be studied or seen again, after two 1,000-foot-high buildings collapse. Both buildings collapse from the fires in them but we're supposed to believe that they found a passport from one of the hijackers intact on the ground that day near the building? There is no footage of another plane hitting the most secure building on Earth? Why? Wouldn't you spend years analyzing what the debris and every other bit of evidence could tell you about what happened? There was an explosion on the ground at Ground Zero that sent smoke billowing up nearly sixty floors from the base of the buildings while they were burning, but it was never reported although it was seen live from Ground Zero. What was that? There are just weird things about what happened, and I think there should be full disclosure.

Of course I know I'm putting my head on the chopping block here, but I don't mind. When change is needed in the world, not enough people voice their opinion and challenge enough. At one point in history, if I'd been sitting here saying the world was round, people would be rolling their eyes. They say believe half of what you see and none of what you hear. Nothing is for sure. I've even heard from a good source that 2+2 actually adds up to a little less than 4 'cause some is lost somewhere in there. Go figure.

North Shore,
O'ahu.

In 1978, when I was six years old, *Jaws* was released,

and I was so terrified I wouldn't swim in the deep end of a pool. That really put a fear of sharks into me. It took me years to get over that, and years after that to learn or even care how many sharks die for their fins, and how important they are to the food chain. When their numbers are imbalanced, other things are imbalanced, and that ultimately affects the whole marine environment. It's the butterfly effect.

That's one of the reasons I am hoping to join Dave Rastovich in doing some work for Sea Shepherd, an organization started by Captain Paul Watson. They've made incredible inroads into stopping daily dolphin slaughters that go on for nearly six months of the year in Japan, the apparently legal killing of well over a quarter of a million baby harp seals in Canada each year, illegal whaling operations in both the Arctic and Antarctic circles, and endless shark finning that happens all over the globe, where the sharks have their fins cut off while they're alive and are just thrown back into the water to drown a slow death.

It's interesting to think about sharks in this context. It seems so much easier to feel protective about dolphins, and not so easy about things that will kill you, particularly if you're a surfer. I have mixed feelings about the great white. It's the ultimate predator. I recently met a guy in California who was attacked by a great white. His back was opened up from his shoulder blade to his butt. I don't know how many stitches were needed to put him back together, but he was up walking around a week or so after the attack. It was frightening to see, but at the same time, I've always had this fascination with the idea of being attacked by a great white and living. Strange.

There is a theme I keep coming back to—where do we draw the line? We've talked about killing animals for food, killing trees for books, polluting the air to make surfboards. There's a theme that runs through our society that human life is worth more than animal life. If you can do the right thing by both, great, but it's humans first. I don't think there are any other animals that think that way. I don't think apes think like that, or dolphins . . . maybe mosquitoes! The only reason I'd kill a shark now is fear for my own life, or for food if my survival depended on it.

North Shore,
O'ahu.

1

2

3

4

I love this angle where you're behind the wave and you can see the curves of the wave almost as they look when you're riding it. This is Pipe and obviously I saw a line to backdoor this section. From here it looks like I'm pulling into a closeout, but those are the best ones, where you go in the wrong way and still get to the other side. Usually at Backdoor you can find right peaks where the angle the waves hit the reef allows you to come from the other side. At Pipe it's not as easy to find them. You need a really peaky, shorter interval swell to find a more broken up wave. In shot 4, if you cut the photo just to the right of me, it looks like I'm pulling into a right going the wrong way! A few years ago, Rob Machado was making a movie of only lefts. To try to make the film, I caught a really good right and went left into the barrel. If he ever finishes that movie maybe that one will make the cut.

5

8

For the love

Why I am who I am

For
the
love

With the children of Momi Village, Fiji.

Al Merrick is one of my favorite people,

and I truly love him like a dad. I called him one time when I was going through a breakup. I was depressed and sad, and Al started talking about God and religion, just for a few seconds. Then he apologized and told me he didn't want to force his beliefs on me, but if I ever wanted to talk about it, he wanted me to feel that was open to me. I thought that was the most loving and kind thing Al could do for me at a difficult time. Al and his wife, Terri, bought me a Bible, and I've read quite a bit of it. There are tremendous lessons for life that you can learn from it. I am not a religious person, per se, but I feel a deep sense of spirituality in my life and connection to people, the world around me and to what is right and wrong or good and bad.

I think a lot of the Bible stories are metaphors, but over the years there have been many powerful people who've used religion in the wrong way, and these things have been distorted. I don't know that I entirely believe the theory of evolution either. I do believe we are spiritual beings, connected by love and disconnected by misunderstanding that we all want the same things for ourselves and others. If God came down and sat next to me, then I'd have my proof of his existence. Until that day happens, I can't say who's right or wrong.

Many different groups of the same religions can have slightly or tremendously differing beliefs, and they all believe they're right, which shows me that they could be all wrong. When you can truly accept everyone for who they are, regardless of their beliefs, that's when you're getting somewhere. There's not a thing in life we don't judge. I feel I'm guided by my conscience, and I search for the meaning in that. Some of my closest friends think I'm too complex in that regard, maybe questioning too many things instead of accepting them, but that's my personality. It's what makes me who I am, and maybe it's also the reason I excel at what I do. I question absolutely everything. I think of every angle and try to see things from different perspectives.

The real healing in life comes through having awareness of other people, no matter who they are or where they've come from. Even Jesus supposedly hung out with prostitutes and murderers and saw past what they did into who they were. That's spirituality to me.

Relaxing at a friend's house in Cocoa Beach, FL.

LEARNING TO ACCEPT WHAT YOU CAN'T CHANGE

I think about death quite often.

I was really scared of it when I was younger. I can't say I'm not scared of it now, but I've gone through periods in my life where I haven't been scared of it at all, where the idea of not being here anymore did not scare me. In fact I felt quite comfortable with the idea. I guess that's what we all need to feel, because we're all going to die.

Maybe that should be taught in schools, how to accept death. Not a scary thing, just realistic. We all need to be able to deal not just with our own deaths but with the deaths of others. Some people say that every fear can be distilled down to a fear of death in its most basic form. When I think about this, I always go back to that game I used to play with Jack Johnson, "You Won't Go."

There's a waterfall that we hike to on the Big Island, where from the platform it's about four hundred feet up and four hundred feet down. You can walk right underneath the waterfall, and a kid we knew slipped and fell and died. I was there one time with a whole bunch of friends, and [former Roxy girl] Sanoe Lake was with us. She stood right under the waterfall, and I was just terrified, thinking she was going to slip and fall. It's really slippery, and if you fall, you die. I have a little bit of a fear of heights, so I got that tingly feeling. Later I imagined being there and falling, and as I fell, calling to my friends, "You won't go!"

That would be a good death. In essence you'd be saying, I'm going to die right now and I'm not afraid, so don't be sad. Maybe the fear of death is really the fear that we haven't achieved the things we wanted to in life—not necessarily the material things, but those regrets about what we didn't do, the people we weren't there for, the conversations we didn't listen to. It's all about what you leave behind, the memory of who you were, and the better that memory, the easier it is to accept dying.

My daughter Taylor is now twelve years old.

While it's not easy to admit, I haven't been there for her as much as I should have, and it's something I think about every single day. My place in her life is somewhere between Kelly and Daddy. In fact I was Kelly-Daddy for a while. If I was a full-time dad, I might feel a bit funny about that—I never called my parents Steve or Judy—but because I'm not there all the time, I guess it makes sense. But I do like it when she calls me Dad.

One of the things that makes me think I must have been good in a past life, or maybe even in this one, is that I have a relationship like the one I now have with Taylor and her family. Things were awkward between her mom and me for a few years, then Tamara married Enzo, and they had two more children. Enzo is a really kind, good-hearted

person who lives for his children. He's enabled me to be as close to Taylor as possible. It had the potential to be awkward for all of us, and it's been nothing like that. From the second I met this guy he treated me like a brother, and maybe with more respect than I sometimes deserved. He said you're welcome in my house 24/7, don't call, don't knock on the door, just come in. I hope he reads this and realizes how much I admire, respect, and love him for that, because it's not something that's easy to express in other ways.

top:
With Taylor, 1998.

left:
With Tamara, Enzo, and their family.

opposite:
KS and PA.

US SURFING SKYBOX

PAMELA

On *Baywatch* **I wasn't even attracted to her.** It was only later when we got to know each other. I was in love at the time, engaged in fact, so I wasn't thinking along those lines. When we got to know each other on a more personal level later, we'd spend time just eating, talking. It was a random kind of relationship, but we had a real understanding of each other. It was a comforting kind of friendship for both of us.

159

Pamela Anderson (actor, friend):

He's just been this little gypsy, in and out of my life, but we became really very close. I have a million love letters from Kelly, and from me to him. It was really a very sweet, very intense relationship. In a sense it never started and it never ended. It just happened from time to time in our lives. He was always there for me in my hard times. The thing I remember quite early in our relationship is that he was very young, and I wanted to get married and have children. I was at that point where I was thinking about that all the time, and we talked about it a lot. But I'm very spontaneous—I went to Cancun, met Tommy Lee, and got married in four days. I was supposed to go to Cocoa Beach from Cancun to meet up with Kelly, but I was married, so that didn't happen.

Sometimes the people you want to hurt the least are the ones you hurt the most. We've been back and forth so many times, it's amazing that he still speaks to me. It's been a strange journey, and I really never wanted to hurt him. I've always said that if you could plant a seed and grow a person, you'd grow Kelly. He's my favorite person in the world, and I've felt so horrible. We've had such intense times.

Some people think that he's flaky, but he's not. He's just on his own time, and I understand that. The problem was that I wanted someone to be around. Even later when I had kids and he took time off the tour and we were together, I didn't want to be that person that took him away from what he loved. With someone who's that talented, you don't want to be the one who's holding him back, but in my case I also didn't want to be the mandatory phone call after the surf contest.

I took him to Tavarua for his birthday. We were there for a week, and it rained and stormed like crazy. We only went surfing once. The rest of the time we were just hanging together, talking, reading, writing, just being together. Of course, when we came back, it just blew up. It had been too intense, but it was wonderful. We still say let's meet up somewhere in ten years, and if we're not with other people, maybe it'll work then. My kids still say to me, "Why can't we marry Kelly?"

Pamela has said a few things in the press or in books that I felt were a little excessive. She went on Howard Stern one time and started talking really personal stuff. I don't know what she was thinking. There are parts of my life that are off-limits, but Pam's boundaries extend beyond those of most humans. For the most part she's been really cool. We've had a couple of relationships, we still have a friendship, and at times we've been very close. She doesn't think bad things about me. She thinks I'm more a victim of her circumstance than the other way around.

Beautiful, famous women come under intense scrutiny. The media around the world sells just that. It's an instinctual feeling among males. I've had some high-profile female friends, and in one case, with Cameron Diaz, a friendship that was seen as something more, but never was. I wish that it hadn't been written about in that way. Cameron has so much scrutiny that it might always be impossible for her to hang out with a friend without this happening. From my perspective, it was a small price to pay for the friendship. She's a good person and a caring friend. I feel quite confident that this is not the way my life is going to be lived in the future. With Pam, I was young and didn't understand the implications of it. The thing is, if you're happy and in love with someone, nothing can take that away. The trick's just finding the right person for the right reasons.

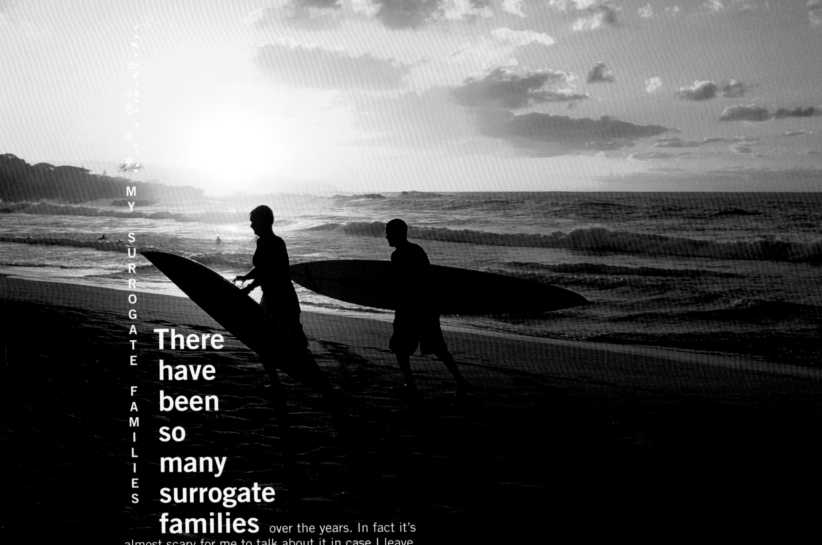

There have been so many surrogate families

over the years. In fact it's almost scary for me to talk about it in case I leave someone out. In Florida my mom was surrogate family to a lot of my friends. She'd pick 'em up from jail or take them to the hospital. They could always talk to my mom. I've always tried to have that same sort of thing on the road wherever I am.

In California, there's the Merricks in Santa Barbara. My friends Ingrid and April Hawkins in Huntington Beach, who took in me and Matty Liu when we were kids; Peggy Rullo, also in Huntington, who was unfortunately murdered when I was about fifteen. The Machados in San Diego, of course, and a recent addition, my girlfriend's family, the Millers, in San Clemente.

In Hawaii, Ronald Hill's family took me in first. That's where I got to know Brock Little, Todd Chesser, Shane Dorian, Ross Williams, and Conan Hayes. The list is endless—there are probably seventy guys who've slept in their house on the floor or on a couch. Then there was Tony and Lee Roy. I stayed with Lee while Tony was in jail for a lot of years. Then the Johnsons. Those three

In Australia, I had the Raymonds, Luke Munro's family on the Gold Coast, the Greens in Torquay, and many others. In France, I stayed with Harry and Sandee Hodge, and now with Pierre and Marianne Agnes. In Jeffreys Bay I've stayed with Robin and Irma Morris for more than ten years. In Tahiti there's the Drollet family and also Raimana's family. Then there's the whole family of Tavarua. And on top of all these, there are many families I've stayed with one or two times. It makes it really hard to leave one and move to another, and of course I can't visit a country without seeing them. It keeps me busy wherever I am.

I hurt my knee when I was seventeen, and it had been bugging me for a few years, particularly right after I won my first world title in 1992. At the beginning of the tour in '93, I was in Australia, staying with the Raymonds, and Bruce took me to a doctor who stuck his fingers into my knee, grabbed my knee cap, and just squashed it. He said, "Okay, we're going into surgery tomorrow."

Bruce dropped me off and picked me up, took me to his house, gave me a bed. Janice brought me food. I don't know how other people feel when they come out of general anesthetic, but you want your mom—you want her to cook your food, turn the TV on, and tell you everything's fine. Janice was there for me then. I feel an affinity for the Raymonds that extends way beyond our business relationship through Quiksilver. They've taken in my friends—friends who are sponsored by other companies, friends who are maybe making a video that Bruce didn't want me to be in. It's put them in a position where, if you were walking along company lines, maybe you wouldn't do it. But Bruce has always opened the door. Janice has always loved having my friends over, loves to entertain and share the homes they're so proud of.

Bruce has always been a father figure to me. We have a professional relationship, too, but Bruce is the kind of guy who sits back and observes, doesn't say a whole lot, thinks it through for a few days, and then tells you what he thinks. I'm always eager to hear what he has to say. He knows me pretty well, Janice maybe a little better. I'm sure they talk about me, and then Bruce delivers the message. I feel that Bruce's advice comes from a pure place, and I've always placed a lot of trust in him.

Janice Raymond, well, she's a mother figure, but she's also like a girlfriend that I can talk to, gossip with, bullshit with. She's not afraid to say anything to me. She calls me out on stuff, and I do the same to her. We have a really close friendship in that way. She's really intrigued by the celebrity life, and she gets all giddy and happy if I have any inside information. We fill a space in each other's lives that no one else could.

Janice Raymond (Australian surrogate mom): I love to gossip and so does Kelly, and I go straight to the guts of the matter with him, like who are you seeing now? I think he was like that with his own mother, too, and he missed that companionship on the tour. I really love his soul. Having such a great talent hasn't really clouded his philosophy of life. He can get on with anybody, and he has this loving, rich soul within. He's got big shoulders, and he loves a lot of people and they return the love. I don't mean since he became champion and famous. He's always been this way. He's got a lot of depth; he's not superficial.

Now that he's a lot older and wiser, he still likes a good gas-bag [gossip session]. He still cares deeply about the people in his life, but he's a be-here-now type of person. He lives in the minute. If I told him I really missed him, I'm sure he'd be there for me, and you know that the missed birthdays don't mean anything. I don't think he's changed, and I think that's why his relationships with rich and famous women don't seem to last. Nothing against any of them, but I suspect there are superficial elements in their lives, and with Kelly there's not.

He never had to open up to me about his relationships. I probe and I get it out of him! Actually he loves it because most people don't dare to ask. I challenged him on my suspicion that he was attracted to the idea of the sex symbol [with Pamela Anderson], and he admitted there was some truth in that. I think Kelly would bring girls around for our approval. He liked to do things as couples. We'd go out for dinner, and he really enjoyed that. He's kind of a sensitive New Age guy, you know. He enjoys talking to women.

One of the things that I really love about Kelly is that he's accepting of his friends and not at all judgmental. He feels quite strongly about how he handles himself in regard to drugs and alcohol, but he never judges others on that. And every now and then he lets his hair down. It's the funniest thing you'll ever see. He'll hassle you for a daquiri! When he first had his apartment in Avalon, he'd be here for dinner almost every night. Lisa [Andersen] was the same. Kelly would never leave the house without a guitar, and I loved that because I always wanted to be that way, too. We'd sing together a lot. I remember him pulling out a guitar at Charles de Gaulle Airport in Paris. We started singing a Sarah McLachlan song, and people thought we were busking and started throwing money at us! They were lovely times.

Sandee Hodge (surrogate mom in France): I think his goal has always been to be like everybody else, to be happy, have a family, and live a normal life. You know, you always want what you haven't got. How many guys would want to be him? Well, I think the reverse often applies to Kelly. The other thing about Kelly that I admire is that most people in the world would be happy to be the best surfer, but he's got his music, his golf . . . He does so many things, and he strives to achieve in so many ways.

Bruce Raymond (Quiksilver executive, mentor): We were at the G-Land surf camp in Java, and Kelly was getting more and more morose. He was telling me how unhappy he was, how he wasn't enjoying the tour anymore, how he felt the other guys on tour weren't his true friends and they were anti-Kelly. I said maybe you're just picking up the vibe that they're sick of you because you're winning everything and you're taking all the energy. They've had enough, so has the media, so you're not feeling the love. It wasn't going to do any of us any good if Kelly had a major meltdown, so I suggested that he step off the tour for a while and then make a comeback. Then everyone would love him for the comeback. He was a bit like, Can I do that? And I said, of course you can. You can turn the burden of your fame into a tool to make the world how you want it.

KS and mom, Judy, share a moment, ASP banquet, Gold Coast.

There was always a funny dichotomy going on with Lisa, who seemed mature beyond her years but also immature half the time. At fifteen she runs away from home and says she's going be the world surfing champion! She wrote her own script and followed it. There's a part of her that had such confidence in what she was doing, and another part that had such a complete lack of confidence. That dichotomy can often create something special in people performance-wise, but it can also cause them problems in their personal lives.

I met Lisa when I was fourteen or so. The first time I remember hanging out with her was the summer of '86, when she was working in the yogurt shop in Huntington Beach, right after she'd run away. She was a couple years older than me, maybe sixteen. I vaguely remembered her from Florida; we were both in Huntington for the summer, so we had stuff in common. She was one of the guys. She was always a cute girl, but the way she acted, the way she surfed, the way she approached life was like a guy. Her confidence came through surfing, while she experienced a lot of problems in her personal life, as I have as well. I saw her go through so many boyfriends. Every time I saw her, it seemed like she was with a new famous or not-so-famous surfer guy. I always thought Lisa was a pretty girl, but there was something so sisterly about her, to me at least, that it would never have worked between us.

We really were like brother and sister. We liked the same music, we drove the same car without knowing the other had it. She didn't know I got a green Mercedes truck the first year it came out with the same interior as hers. It was crazy. I'd see her after a while, and we're riding the same boards.

As a surfer she blew me away. She absorbed the way guys ride waves, but when she did it she had a feminine feel. She'd do a masculine bottom turn and an off-the-top, but somehow it had woman written all over it. Her surfing allowed her to be who she really was.

With Lisa Andersen at Surfer Poll Awards.

L I S A

 **Lisa Andersen (4x world surfing champion, friend):** I was in the room the first time Kelly picked up a guitar. Of course I wasn't thinking back then that one day I'd be saying that about the eight-time world champion. We were young, and we got stuck traveling together a lot, mainly because the men's and women's tour were often in the same place. We'd have to share a chaperone and a car. So I spent a lot of time waiting for Kelly—waiting in the car, waiting at the airport, waiting at the hotel. He always took his time.

The incredible thing about Kelly is that everything he touched, he lit up. It seemed like he could do anything. He was really smart with math problems, he could debate politics with anyone, except me. I wouldn't go there.

I've always had an interest in women's surfing, not just Lisa. As a kid I thought Frieda Zamba was amazing. She won four world titles, so she must have been. I'm sure she could have won more, but she stopped to have a family. She was an impressive, aggressive, strong surfer. I'm impressed by what Margo Oberg did long before Frieda. I've surfed with Kim Mearig at Rincon over the years and thought she was like a female Curren, the way she linked her turns so seamlessly. Then there's Layne Beachley. In 1992 she went out in a men's expression session at Lacanau, France. I was still in the contest, so I didn't surf in the expression session. I was sitting with [surfer and writer] Derek Hynd watching, and she did a couple of turns where Derek and I looked at each other and went, Are you kidding? That was really a monumental change in the way a woman surfed the face of a wave.

When a woman really charges, it catches people off-guard. Chelsea Georgeson is like that, so are Stephanie Gilmore and Sofia Milanovich. Carissa Moore is going to be like that. She can throw airs and tail slides and pull into the barrel—she's the real deal. It'll be interesting to see what happens when she gets to her full-grown size. She's always been a cute surfer, but now she's going to be powerful. She'll probably have to change her style to suit her body type. Right now she rides from the tail and just whips it around, which is very cool to watch.

We had this weird brother/sister relationship. I often felt he was annoyed by me being around, and he could be quite arrogant about it. I never knew if it was because I was a girl or something more. I never had a crush on him, never. Which was interesting because he was such an attractive person, and so many girls thought he was the coolest thing in the world. I just didn't buy it; he was my brother. I admired him a hell of a lot, and I emulated the things he did, without being too obvious, like his preparation for an event. You could watch and learn so much. There was also a little bit of jealousy going on there. We were with the same sponsor, and you could measure the attention you got against the other.

When we were both world champions, we had some amazing times together. One trip to Tahiti we even shared a bunk, which got people talking. I'd get that all the time—what's the deal with you and Kelly? Are you hooked up? I used to laugh so hard about that. We had enough ups and downs in our relationship without having that happen!

I think the only thing you could say maybe Kelly isn't really good at is his choice of women. I mean, it's none of my business, but he's such a great guy, so talented and so warm and generous, you'd think that he'd meet the best girl in the world. I've always wanted that for him 'cause I know there's one out there—sorry I'm already taken! Girls are so drawn to him because he's kind of mysterious, and they want to know what he's about. And I don't know, he just attracts these train wrecks! I shouldn't talk, I've had a few myself.

I remember at G-Land years ago he was wandering around with this big smile on his face, and he came up to me and told me he was going to be a dad. I was the first person he told—I guess because as a surfer and a mom I could relate. I thought he'd make an amazing father because he's so good with kids, especially with Erica [Lisa's daughter], who grew up on tour. He was Uncle Kelly, and he always had time for her. I thought he'd have tons of kids by now, but he's got Taylor and they have a special relationship.

You know, deep down I think Kelly loves the screaming girls, the adulation. I've been with him in malls where it's like Beatlemania, and I'm thinking, How the hell can he handle that! He says he hates it, but I think he feeds off of it. He loves being the center of attention, and I think he channels that into his success. One of the biggest fears men have is of losing their hair, right? Look at how Kelly handled that one! Have you ever seen anyone so completely confident in being bald! And he's still beautiful.

A lot of people have taught me

how to live. Obviously my mom. She's taught me most of what I've learnt in life. But there are other people who've taught me profound things. Al Merrick taught me to be nonjudgmental and kind. Bruce Raymond has taught me a lot about waiting and watching before deciding. A lot of that pertains to business but also to the personal. Peff Eick has taught me a lot about contentment in life, about surrounding yourself with the right people who you know are good for you, and not hiding away in a bubble. Peff and the Johnsons together have been a really strong influence on the way I see life. They've taught me so much about the importance of family.

Many people in America don't know

TREVOR HENDY

who Trevor is, but in Australia he's a sporting icon, one of the greatest ironmen of the surf lifesaving movement. Moreover, he's a great all-round waterman and someone who thinks deeply about life. Trevor and the people he works with led me to a greater understanding of myself in a very short period of time. I've been able to share much more openly with people since then. I can honestly say that through my friendship with Trevor I've had some of the most profound experiences I've had in my life. The idea is that you never stop learning, you never stop growing as a person, and you never close your mind to what is possible for you and for other people. When you adopt that approach you become more of an observer, and you become better able to help other people. When you stop learning, you grow old and you die, because life is learning.

Peff Eick (friend, mentor): I think I have a special role in his life. Kelly listens to me, and we talk about a lot of stuff. I've been married for thirty-six years, he knows my daughters, he knows my grandchildren, and I think he feels an integral part of my family. Because of that I think he'll discuss things with me that he doesn't discuss with a lot of others, about his goals and ambitions, his love life. We'll get in a car and drive to a golf course, and it'll take an hour, which is about as long as it takes in a car for the conversation to go somewhere deep and complex, and ours usually does. I don't know that I know more about Kelly than anybody else, but he's like a son to me. I listen to his struggles in life, the kind that everybody has, and I empathize.

I think it's hard to be any celebrity, and by the way, all the celebrities I've met in my life I've met through Kelly! Eddie Vedder, Jack Johnson, now that he's found fame. I think it's a struggle for all these guys because the public want so much out of them. I think Kelly deals with it beautifully. He's a great representative of surfing. He always presents with intelligence and dignity, he's great with kids. I saw him walk over at Sunset Beach one day and give his board to this kid. He'll do things like that. We were sitting on my deck one day looking out over Pipeline, and these two kids wander along the beach about fifteen feet away. One of them says, Oh, you're Kelly Slater. Kelly goes, yeah. The kid says, Can I have your autograph? Kelly says, yeah, just a minute. And he jumps up, runs into the house, gets a pen and a piece of paper, and takes it out onto the beach and gives the kid his autograph. I mean, who does that? He takes his position responsibly.

I think if you hung around with Kelly for a short while, and you didn't know who he was, you'd quickly figure out that this guy has some special talents, that he's not quite like everyone else. I don't know how you would see that, but you would.

above: With Peff Eick.

right: Miki Dora in his prime.

I played golf with Miki three or four times

and every one was a beautiful story. Somewhere I have the only photo ever taken of Miki playing golf. I hid the camera from him, and then snapped a shot from the golf cart right behind him. The most horrible golf swing, fundamentally one of the worst swings you'll ever see, but the ball is going straight. That was in Biarritz, the last time I played with him before he died. It was a foursome, me and Miki, Stephen Bell and Bruce Raymond. At the end of the round Bruce had the scorecard, and he passed it to me to sign. He was going to get us all to sign it, but I knew there was no way Miki would sign.

The first time I met Miki in South Africa, I asked him to sign an autograph for my little brother, and he said he liked me, but he just couldn't. He said, "The fucking Japanese think my autograph is worth $5,000 and I can't let 'em down." But now Bruce goes, "Don't worry, he'll sign the scorecard. All gentlemen sign their scorecards." So I signed and passed it on to Miki, and Bruce asks him to sign it. Miki says he can't; Bruce tells him all gentlemen sign their scorecards. Then Miki goes, "Who's going to end up with it?" In the end he reluctantly signed it, and Bruce now has the card framed on his wall.

As we were leaving the course that day, I noticed how old and beaten up Miki's clubs were. I told him I had a friend who could organize a new set for him. He goes, "Don't promise me that if you're not going to do it." I said I meant it and that I'd organize it. I got back to California, and he sends me a fax, saying the same thing—don't tell me you're going to get them if you're not. I faxed back—Miki, you'll get your clubs, and I don't want to hear from you until you do. I got the clubs and sent them to him. When he got the clubs, he faxed me again to thank me, and he signed the fax. I still have it.

Harry Hodge (former Quiksilver executive, friend): Kelly stayed with us in France four or five seasons. He felt very comfortable in the compound and having kids around. No threats, no demands, and he could do whatever he wanted. We didn't want to bother him about coming over for dinner every night, but he'd just show up and we'd drink red wine and get relaxed. He'd play golf, bring friends around. We know a lot of surfers, and their lives revolve around surfing, whereas Kelly, like Miki Dora, really made an effort to step outside of that. I think he's also like Miki in the way that he goes into hiding from his own celebrity from time to time—because everyone wants a piece of you. I guess that's why they got on so well.

MARK RICHARDS

I love to read or hear whatever MR says

because he's such a humble guy, but what strikes me most is when he talks about competition. He has a broad overview of it, but also such a vast personal experience as a competitor. And, although he's humble, he still has the ego of a competitor, which is to say—this is mine, I deserve to have it! When it comes to his assessment of me as a competitor, I agree that in some respects we're similar and in others not. He would argue with me on this, but as I've often said, distraction during a contest can actually cause me to refocus on winning. Unfortunately I never really saw MR in his competitive career. Maybe in tiny waves in Florida when I was a little kid. I'd get to Hawaii right after Pipe finished every year when I was young, and I'd miss the Triple Crown, so while I was there for the last few years he was competing, I never got to see him. That's a regret.

Mark Richards (4x world surfing champion, inspiration): When I came along on a twin fin, my attitude was, I'm going to show these guys where you can go on a wave. And I did. Kelly did the same thing with his approach, and he has never sat back and gone, well, that's as far as I can go. He always wants to go further, and that's his greatness. You know when you used to sit in school doodling these stick men carving impossible turns, or getting barreled backward? Well, he's taken those doodle dreams and turned them into reality.

right: With Shane Dorian.

below left: Mark Richards and KS at a charity fundraiser.

below right: Richards at Off The Wall, 1976.

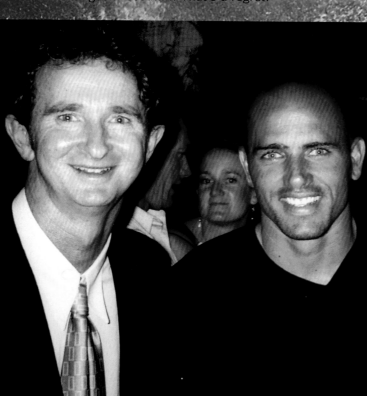

Shane's probably the biggest influence on my surfing

since my professional career started. We've been surfing together since we were twelve years old, and I think we look at waves in a similar way. Shane has probably charged big waves more than I have, but we've really pushed each other in all kinds of conditions. We were great travel partners because we didn't like the same girls, but we kinda did, so we'd both end up happy. In surfing, I think we had the same attitude, in that we'd look at a big wave as we would a small wave, or a gnarly wave as we would a fun wave.

The biggest days I've ever surfed have been with Shane, whether it's paddling or towing, from Jaws to Waimea to Himalayas to Cloudbreak. We've always been able to rely on each other. We had a full-moon session at Restaurants a few years ago. It was double overhead on the sets, and we surfed from ten to midnight on the brightest moon I've ever seen. It was the closest the moon had been to Earth in hundreds of years or something like that, and there was a huge ring around it. We surfed it on soft-top Morey Doyles, and we were noseriding waves together and grabbing the rails and pulling into the barrel together. It was one of the most insane surfs I've ever had and maybe the most memorable.

Shane has always been a guy who knows what he wants in life and goes and gets it. The only thing I ever knew I wanted for sure was a world title, but Shane knew where he wanted to live, he knew the house he wanted to build, the girl he wanted to marry. He's been an inspiration to me in that way.

Shane Dorian (surfer, friend):

Kelly's good points are that he's compassionate, intelligent, great at giving advice, honest, competitive, trusting, thoughtful, analytical, has a major weakness for beautiful women. His bad points are that he's always late, too trusting, bad at taking advice, overly competitive, overly analytical, and he has a major weakness for beautiful women.

The best time I ever had with Kelly was in the late 1990s when we were traveling together on the tour. We had both just become single and were really in the exact same frame of mind. We spent the year doing lots of wild stuff that was out of character for both of us, and we became closer than we had ever been. We had no reason to go home, so we would just float from country to country having a blast. We were totally not focused on competing, going out all night when we had early heats, but for some reason we both did really well that year.

I hope Kelly finds someone deserving to share his life with. Someone who brings out the best in him, who wants him but doesn't need him. Kelly has never really had a home since high school, so it will be great to see him put some roots down and have a home base and a family. He has achieved so much in his career, but I think he knows that that stuff will pale in comparison with having his own little family that loves him just for being himself.

I met Jeni and Al Hing

from the Sunshine Coast in Australia in '93 when they were honeymooning in Tavarua. We hit it off, and we've been friends ever since. When Steve Irwin started to get popular on TV, my brother Stephen and I loved to watch him. We'd imitate his voice, "Oh mate, she's a little bewdy!" We'd watch his show every day in Hawaii and get right into it. I was just a fan. It was only years later that I realized he lived quite close to the Hings, so I asked Jeni if she knew him. It turns out she grew up with the guy, and he was a good friend. I was like, wow, can we meet him? She said all you had to do was ask.

Stephen was up that way, surfing in Noosa, so Jeni hooked up Stephen and Steve to go surfing. They hit it off right away because Stephen grew up camping and fishing and messing around in boats. I came up a few days later and met Steve and his family at their Australia Zoo. We went straight to see Harriet the tortoise, who was 171 years old at the time, taken from Galapagos by the Darwin expedition when she was 4 years old. She just loved eating hibiscus flowers, but when you fed her, you had to get your fingers out of the way real quick.

Next we're hand-feeding alligators. Steve says, "You've watched the shows, you know what to do. Get in here!" I mean, there's watching and there's doing, and they're quite different. I had white socks on, and we were feeding them chicken, which is also white, so the things start coming after my legs. I had to jump back over the fence three or four times. Steve's scratching his head trying to figure it out, then he goes, "Aw mate, take your shoes and socks off." Then it worked fine.

I don't think it was as risky for him as it looked. He knew those animals so well, their exact movements and characteristics. I think at the time he had 105 crocs and alligators in his zoo. We met Steve's friend Wes, who nearly lost his life when a croc had him in its jaws. He was badly injured but got away briefly. The croc was just about to take him by the head when Steve managed to distract it and get him out of the way. They lived on the edge, but it was an edge they knew very well. I would equate it to riding huge surf. You're relatively safe if you know what you're doing, but you are also close to a lot of wave energy and it's a little terrifying—otherwise you wouldn't be doing it.

Ironically, right before Steve died, I was going to go to Australia and get to spend a little time with him. I saw him in March and told him I'd try to get back in August to do a trip. He died in September so I could have been on that same trip. Quite a strange feeling. Makes you think things could've and might've been different.

You could argue that Steve made his living off of animals in captivity, and I feel quite strongly about some animals in captivity, say dolphins. Alligators and crocs have been somewhat demonized, so it's hard to think of them in the same way. Dolphins are beautiful, crocs want to kill you. But I have zero doubt in my mind about where Steve's heart was in respect to the animals he worked with. He did more for animals in Australia than any other person. He gave a significant percentage of his income to buy land so that endangered wombats could be protected. He'd fly animals from one place to another so that they could live in peace. He thought it was absurd that people would kill these rare and beautiful animals for food, but at the same

With the late Steve Irwin at Australia Zoo.

Tom Carroll (world champion surfer, friend):

I narrowly missed my third world title in 1988, and in '89 I had a terrible year, just a downward spiral. When Kelly joined Quiksilver [in 1990], it gave me a new lease on life in many ways. We had a vibrant, full, and broad relationship right from the start. I mean you'd have to have significant issues within yourself to take exception to Kelly, even if you considered him a rival. He's got a great mind, and if you close yourself off to that, then you're missing out. In many ways Kelly is a people-pleaser. That's one of the nice things about him, but maybe not always so nice for him. I think he needs to be careful of that. He really does care for people, he's very sensitive, as you'd have to be to reach his level of achievement. He's in touch with so many people across such a broad spectrum. He's a world person, not an American. In fact that's going to be another challenge for him when the time comes to sit down in one place and call it home. But he loves a challenge, and he'll deal with it.

His emotional intelligence is what I find inspirational about him. He has the ability to break down and be human, just break down and let it go. I've always been frightened of that, never knew how to do it. It was always like, hold it together, buddy, or you're fucked! That only works for so long. I'm not quite sure how to put this, but most men simply don't have that. He has the emotional scope of a female. It's quite extraordinary, and I think it's been a factor in his string of world titles. He doesn't exist in this simple state of happy or sad, it's much more complex than that, and he knows where to go to draw on that emotional energy when he needs it. It's what has enabled him to stay hungry and to keep reinventing himself all these years.

time he understood and respected the traditions of indigenous people who lived off the land.

In a phone conversation one night he asked me, "Are you ready to step it up to the next level, mate?" I asked him what he meant, and he said, "Are you ready to hand-feed the big croc?" It was a thirteen-footer, he said. I was going up to see him in a couple of days, and I had nightmares about it each night until I went. I'd just read in the newspaper that he was really mad at the prime minister of Australia because there'd been a meeting of heads of state, and on the menu was emu steak and crocodile tails. Steve was quoted in the newspaper as telling the prime minister, "Get an act, will ya!"

When I asked him about it, he said, "It's like you're in America, and the president serves bald eagle." So I took him on a bit and I said, You know, bald eagle's not bad but manatee is even better! He went very quiet. Then finally he laughed, "Aw mate, ya got me a bewdy!"

Steve really cared about every animal's role in the ecosystem. Right before he died he spent six weeks tagging crocs, helping to find out more about their migratory patterns. He was as passionate about animals as anyone on Earth. I was devastated beyond words when Steve died. Like a lot of people who got to know him just a little, I felt robbed. He was truly one of my all-time heroes.

this page, clockwise from top left: With Christian Hosoi; wrestling with Tom Carroll; Tavarua party with Julia Roberts and Jon Roseman; with Barracuda and family in Momi Village, Fiji; being silly with Kalani; with Dad, Sean, and Stephen.

this page, clockwise from top left: With a buddy at Steve Irwin's Australia Zoo; Kelly Lager, taste the difference; celebrating seven; folks back in the day, Judy and Steve Slater; another furry friend at Australia Zoo; Mom in two minds at Australia Zoo.

5

6

7

8

This is J-Bay in July '07. I stayed for about two weeks after the tour event had ended in really small, frustrating surf on the second-to-last day of the waiting period. The last day of the waiting period was forecast to be bad but ended up really good and most people were leaving. This was the first of two or three good swells we enjoyed over that period, and this is one of about a thousand off-the-tops I did during it. At J-Bay it can be tricky to fit in a really good turn and not get passed up by the wave. I just barely finish this one before the wave tried to sneak past me. I find that you want to try and surf ahead of where you think you need to be here, and then it starts to look like your timing is right. That way you can use the whole face and not be stuck near the pocket trying to catch up.

13

14

15

16

For the fans

**88
questions
for
Kelly.**

Inundated,
Huntington
Beach,
California.

1

When did you first become hooked on surfing?

It was really just a summertime thing for me from when I was about five years old.

2

What is it about surfing that you love?

I love the speed, I love drawing lines. I think even from a young age it was about drawing a line on the face of a wave that meant something to me.

3

Were you encouraged to surf by your family?

I was encouraged but never pushed

4

How much time would you average at the beach growing up?

After school I'd generally go straight to the beach and surf if there were any kind of waves at all, but I was involved in other things, too, like tennis, football, basketball. I'd do stuff with my friends, like wakeboarding, fishing. So it wasn't surf all the time but definitely the majority of my time.

5

If you weren't a pro surfer, what would you have been?

I've always loved music, and as a kid I wanted to be a comedian, so that's what I would have said back then. Maybe now I'd say alternative medicine, but it didn't appeal to me until I was in my twenties. Music's still there of course, and I also have a kind of closet love for architecture.

6

Describe Cocoa Beach where you grew up.

A small town that had big dreams and potential at one point but never quite got there, but a very loyal community. Everyone seems to end up back there at some point in their lives. It's kind of your typical small town.

7

What did you dream about as a grom?

I used to watch waves and dream about drawing different lines on them. I'd imagine what Tom Curren would do on that wave.

8

Did you ever get the feeling that you were the chosen one?

It's a little strange to talk about that, but I've always had this inner feeling that things were going to go my way. My mom has always mentioned this feeling she had when I was born about what was going to happen in my life.

9

What sort of kid were you?

Until I was eight I was bigger than most of the other kids in my class and kind of pudgy. I had this fear that I was going to grow up fat. It really concerned me. I wasn't really fat but I looked like a bully, so that's what I became. I was the one running the class. I wouldn't classify myself as rebellious, but I was certainly angry, and that lasted until about eight or nine years old, when I just became much mellower.

10

Was surfing an escape for you?

It definitely was, but I only realized that later.

11

When did you realize that surfing was something you could possibly do for a living?

When I was about twelve years old. I won a ticket to Hawaii in a contest, and the reality of it dawned on me.

12

How difficult was the amateur circuit?

I always felt there was room to breathe there. I surfed to the best of my ability and to my best understanding of the system, and I won quite a bit.

13

How much of your ability is inherited and how much is practice?

I can't say my dad was a great surfer. In fact I can't even say he was a good surfer, but he had a good mind for things, and my mom was a tough competitor. I figured out a lot just by observing everyone. I don't practice a lot nowadays. It always takes me a couple of sessions to get back to my best

if I haven't surfed for a while, but then it seems to come pretty quick. I do sometimes show up at events where I haven't surfed for three weeks, and I'll jump in a heat on a new board. There's a subconscious part of me that likes that challenge. It awakens me somehow and gets me back in the right frame of mind.

14

What is the right body type for surfing?

For my generation and the way we surf, it seems you don't want to be too overly muscular, but you also don't want to be tall and gangly. In the 1970s, guys like Nat Young, Michael Peterson, and Mark Richards were quite long and thin, then as the equipment changed, the ideal body shape changed. Tom Carroll was able to do what he did through sheer strength, but at times I think he may have been too muscular. For our generation it seems that five-eight to five-ten seems to be the magic number, and strong and fit without being overly muscular. Surfing's that fine line between strength and grace.

15

How much did Tom Curren influence you?

Oh, far greater than anyone else. Probably as much of an influence as everyone else put together. I based my surfing on Tom when I was riding the face and on Pottz when I was doing airs.

16

Outside of surfing, which elite athletes did you look up to?

I love watching great athletes in their prime. Loved to watch Tyson, Jordan; love watching Tiger now. Federer's almost not fun to watch because he's so much better than everyone that you get the sense no one will beat him. But no one athlete ever meant as much to me when I was growing up as, say, Tom Curren or Buttons [Montgomery Kaluhiokalani].

17

Who was the hardest surfer to compete against when you were a junior?

Probably Shane Beschen. We had a full-on rivalry going from a fairly young age. We were also pretty good friends, but almost every time we met I got the better of him. Although it was much closer than looking at the results now would have you believe.

179

18

How excited were you when you got your first sponsors?

Oh, very. The idea of being sponsored was with me from the beginning. My mom and dad always liked to tell the story of when I got one of my first boards, and all I wanted was to have "team" written on it, so I could feel like I was part of something.

19

When did you get your first article in a surf magazine?

My first picture in any kind of magazine was when I was ten, and I got a picture in the local paper that same year. I was in a national magazine, *Surfing,* when I was twelve. It was like a third of a page in black-and-white, taken at the Sundek Classic in Florida.

20

First cover or spread?

First cover was *East Coast Surfer,* which was an insert east of the Mississippi in *Surfer* when I was maybe fourteen. My first real cover was *Surfing* when I was fifteen, doing an air at Sebastian Inlet.

21

What were Slater family holidays like when you were young?

Generally we'd go to my cousins' house up in Maryland. We'd go for Christmas and sometimes in the summer. They were the only family holidays. My dad would get drunk, and we'd wrestle with him. I remember one time I headbutted him in the eye, and he needed stitches. It scared me to death to see him bleeding like that. In my mind they were fun times, hanging with my cousins, but they were also scary times with my parents not really getting along.

22

If you had your life over again, would you do it all the same?

If you had the awareness that you have now, you'd always do some things differently. There are things that I've done that I regret. There are choices that I've made that have adversely affected other people who matter to me a great deal. If I could change those things, I definitely would.

23

Do you remain in contact with childhood friends?

Oh yeah, lots of them. In fact, just last year I got in touch with a kid I hadn't seen since third grade.

24

How did you manage not to get distracted by girls?

Are you joking? Well, early on it was easy because I didn't care, but I've always been distracted by girls.

25

Who was the local surfer you admired most when growing up?

Matt Kechele. He brought the world home to me and my brother Sean through videos and word of mouth, and he also took us to the world.

26

Why was that wave on Pipe in '91 so important?

Because up to that point there was a lot of pressure on me about whether or not I would charge, whether I'd go for it. It was the chink in my armor in some people's eyes. To me that wave symbolized "I'll go," as opposed to "you won't go."

27

When did you realize you were going to win your first world title?

I think I took the lead in the rankings when I beat Gary Elkerton at Hossegor [in the Rip Curl Pro]. After two events that year I was in fourth place, and I realized that winning the title was possible. I felt like I hadn't really surfed well yet, but I was beating the top guys. But after Hossegor I really buckled down to win it.

Kelly Slater
U ARE So pride. STAY with your
Silicon Valley bitchs!!

Kelly Slater

5151 1501 0000 0011
5151
VALID THRU 01/08
ROBERT KELLY SLATER

Debit
MasterCard

Stalker's
revenge.
Hossegor,
France.

28

How important was winning the Quiksilver in Memory of Eddie Aikau?

It wasn't something like I felt I had to do to top off my career or anything like that. It was more personally fulfilling than important career-wise.

29

What other things in life have you missed out on because of your focus on surfing?

All my friends went away to college, and for quite a few years I really felt like I had missed out. It wasn't so much that I loved school, but I loved the friends I had, and I felt I missed out by not doing what they did.

30

Did the flak about being a small-wave surfer ever affect you?

When I was younger and the pressure was on, but after getting used to Pipe and getting some good, big ones under my belt, especially that one in '91, I didn't feel the pressure to have to prove anything like I had before.

31

At what stages of your career have you felt you were at your peak?

Probably '96 and '97, then again in '03 and '05. I feel that the best surfing I've done was in '03, and I've touched on that level again a few times for an event. The best I've ever surfed in an event start to finish was J-Bay '05, but there was a period in '03, from J-Bay right through to Brazil, where I felt more solid and confident than ever, and my mind was in the right place. I'd started doing metaphysical work, and I was opening my mind up to a wider understanding of the world. I'd begun to listen to people's feelings rather than just their words, and it was really helping me. I think any athlete who reaches a certain age will start to feel the increasing physical challenge of what he does, but I believe the emotional and mental side of it is even more important. People who keep raising the bar as they get older generally do so because they keep themselves emotionally and mentally young and are aware and open to change. That's how you keep it fresh and exciting. If it's not fresh and exciting, you should end your career.

32

Which victory is the most special to you?

That's a tough one. Probably Pipeline Masters '95. Pipe '98 was great, too, but looking back on '95, it was just so well scripted. It was this great battle between me and my greatest friends on tour, Rob Machado and Sunny Garcia, in Sunny's backyard. All the elements came together with Sunny potentially winning the world title that day, Occy on his comeback . . . just so much going on.

33

Your thoughts on Andy Irons?

He's so driven as a competitor. I see parts of myself in that, particularly early in my career, and I see parts of my brother Sean in him, too. I guess that comes from Andy being the older brother in his family. When I was first on tour with Andy, I gravitated toward him, wanted to be close with him, and I feel like I really tried and he just wasn't open to it. I was the enemy, and you can't be close to the enemy. There's been a lot said about our rivalry, some of it blown out of all proportion, some of it not far from the truth. It's gotten pretty intense between us in and out of the water at times, but my personal belief is that any two people can get along, no matter what the circumstances, if just one of them is willing to let that happen. Things might be different between us when we're both not on the tour. I can certainly say that Andy has pushed me to greater heights.

34

Who was the hardest competitor you faced?

Tom Curren. I surfed against him eight times before I beat him. I'm not sure that was because he was such a great competitor; I think it was because he was such a great surfer he didn't have to worry about [how he competed]. I had a mental block about beating him, just couldn't do it.

35

Has there been a final you didn't make and wished you had?

Yes, two of them specifically—'91 and '98 Pipe Masters. Ninety-one was the first time Tom Carroll won and my first year in the event. I narrowly lost in the semis and was torn apart watching that final unfold from the beach, but it was also probably the best heat I've ever watched. In '98, I was with Jake Paterson in the semi and needed, like, a three-point ride to make the final. I'd already sealed the world title by making the semi, and I needed this one wave with six minutes to go and I couldn't get it. I can generally find a three at Pipeline with ten seconds to go, but not on this occasion. I'd won the title and lost my edge, lost my concentration. The celebration had already begun. So Jake took me out, and there was a sense

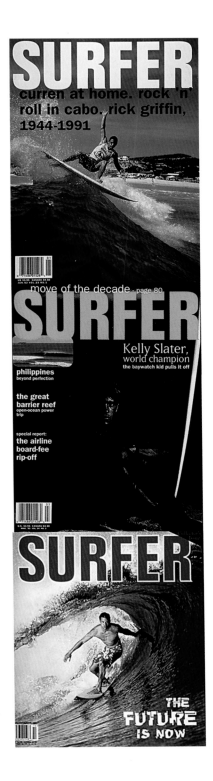

of Aussie retribution about it because I'd already taken out Mick Campbell and Danny Wills. Jake and I are friends, but he had a bone to pick with me that day. It inspired him to one of the greatest wins I've seen at Pipeline. He came out of the barrel on the buzzer to score a ten and win the final.

36
What was your most satisfying world title win?

Oh, '98 was pretty special, but then my seventh in '05 was kind of amazing, too. That was the most emotional I ever felt winning a title, but it was beyond my control at the end in Brazil. Whereas in '98 it was all on the line at Pipeline.

37
Which title was the hardest?

It seems like '06 was the easiest, while '95 and '98 were both hard, but '95 was probably the hardest.

38
Do you consider yourself lucky with injuries?

For the most part, yes. I've never had one put me out for more than one event. I did have a knee injury that nagged me for about three or four years early in my career, but I'd say I've been one of the luckier athletes in surfing.

39
Do you go into each heat with a plan?

If I'm really focused, I do, but I've surfed so many heats without a plan.

40
Do you have any superstitions?

I've had them about the wax I use and my little pre-heat routine and so on. But when I surfed at my best, around '03, I began to realize that superstitions are so limiting, despite any focus they give you. If you don't do what you're supposed to do, you'll remember and go, "Oh shit, I forgot to do that." When I broke it down and looked at the whole superstition thing and its effect on performance, I understood what Stevie Wonder meant when he wrote "Superstition." That's what they do to you. Mine were pretty basic things, like using the same block of wax throughout the contest, doing a certain routine before I surf, I have to be the first guy in the water, or I don't—just these mind games. The good side of superstitions is that they can focus you. The bad side is that you can get stuck in your mind.

41
Is it difficult to focus at contests?

It can be, particularly if there are a lot of people in your face. I tend to shut down to the people closest to me during

a contest. As a general rule of thumb, if I tune out to you during a contest, I probably really care about you. For years I went through this thing where I would not talk to my mom for the duration of a contest. Sometimes I'd call her five minutes before my first heat, but then she wouldn't hear from me until I was done, even if it was two weeks. It was kind of a double superstition because she believed it, too, that it would make me lose focus, but it was really pretty silly.

42
Have you changed your competitive strategy over the years?

I'm on the best waves, I'm maximizing my scores, and I'm looking at what I can do to get on top of my competitor. For example, if the other guy gets a good wave, I try to get a better one right behind it, then get back out there and get priority. That can be a mortal wound to a competitor. On the flip side of that, if someone does that to me, I'll try to immediately come back from it with more energy.

43
How has the standard of surfing changed over your time on tour?

Watch videos from the early '90s and from today. The contrast is drastic. There are two generations in there, but it looks more like four.

Another
year,
another
autograph.
Hossegor,
France.

44

Do you feel you have any competitive weaknesses?

I can be unprepared, that's probably my biggest weakness. It's more physical than mental. I'll show up and won't be in the best shape. I generally eat well, but I might show up late and not know too much about the conditions or which board is going to work best. I'll be in a scramble and need to rely on prior knowledge of the place we're surfing.

45

Do you feel you have a "home court" advantage at most places by now?

Every sport has a home court advantage, and for me it gets down to the support you feel from people in that place. I feel like I have a charmed life in that I have a home everywhere I go, and that's my home court. Even when I'm in Australia surfing against an Australian, I feel confident and comfortable. It is hard surfing against the best guy at a particular break, say Mick Fanning or Parko or Dean Morrison at Snapper, and if you beat them, it's a huge boost.

46

Are you a last-minute man?

Do you get anxious coming down to the last few minutes?

There's definitely been a pattern in my career of me coming from behind at the end of heats and events and years. I did it much more at the beginning of my career, and as I got older I became more comfortable controlling a heat from the start. But early on I relied on more of a knockout method at the end of a heat than winning rounds from the beginning. I might get a little nervous toward the end of a heat if I'm behind, but I usually process it fairly well and get to a place where I can do what I need to do to win.

47

Do you still make mistakes in heats?

Absolutely. In '03, surfing against Phil McDonald in the Quiksilver Pro France, he needed a 7.8 or something like that. Five minutes left in the semifinal, and I had priority, and I was sitting closer to the shoulder. A wave came and it didn't look very good, so I pulled back and let him take off deep. I could probably argue that that single wave cost me the world title that year. Pretty much every heat I lost this year [in 2007] I can find some sort of mistake behind it, and that's probably true for most everyone. Whoever makes fewer mistakes most often wins in competition. Of course, you can always make mistakes and still outsurf someone for a win, or not make a mistake and get outsurfed, too.

48

In surfing, how much is physical and how much is mental?

For me, the classic example would be Nathan Hedge beating Andy Irons in Brazil in '05, which gave me world title number seven. Hedgy went out there with a strict game plan, and he stuck to it. I don't think I've ever seen anyone so focused on a plan of how to win a heat. He dominated the heat, and I really believe that almost anyone else surfing against Andy in that heat would have been blown out of the water.

49

Did he do it for you or for Hedgy?

I think he did it for both of us. Hedgy and I have an interesting friendship, and at times it's almost been brotherly, where I felt he really wanted to show me something. It might be to blow me out of the water or do me a favor, and in a way it's the same thing. He beat me at J-Bay in '04 fair and square, and maybe he was completing something in Brazil.

50

How much of your surfing is

for fun and how much is practice?

My life is pretty busy, I have a lot of things I'm doing, I travel a lot, and I don't put as many hours in the water as I used to. A lot of that time in the water is on photo shoots or getting ready for an event. Unfortunately, only a small part of it is purely for enjoyment without any of that. I like to think I surf more for enjoyment than for preparation, and I'm lucky in that I can go out and enjoy myself and be working at the same time.

51

Do you ever focus on one maneuver when you're surfing?

I have done, but I get kinda ADD. Occasionally, if the waves are repeating themselves enough, I'll just concentrate on an air or carve or something. At Pipeline I'll go out and practice getting barreled, over and over, but with different takeoff lines.

52

Do you surf better free-surfing or in heats?

I think a lot of my best surfing has been done in heats. I tend to rise to my best in a contest environment.

53

What's the most radical move you've ever done that no one has seen?

Probably rodeo clowns, airs which I've never completed on film yet.

54

Are there still times when you surprise yourself surfing?

Mmm, I surprise myself in a negative way sometimes. I'll come through a section and fall off and think, How many times have I done that the right way? Sometimes I'm baffled that I don't correct a mistake before it happens. That happens more than being surprised at something I make. There are occasions, of course, when I've had that sensation of making something work that I didn't expect to, but at the same time if you try it, you expect to make it at some point.

55

What move gives you the most satisfaction?

Probably a big barrel.

56

How has personal self-improvement affected your performance?

In a nutshell, I think the more receptive you are to changing yourself, the better you're going to be at everything in life—the better friend you'll be, the better partner you'll be. The more you can open your mind and get rid of the filters you have between information and thought, the better in life you'll do.

57

When are you happiest?

When I have nothing on my plate, I surf my brains out all day long, have a good meal, and listen to music and talk about life with my friends in some comfortable place.

58

What are the most valuable lessons you've learned in life?

Honesty is the best policy. It really is true. Almost all of us are in denial of where we are in life, at some level. The reality of your situation is usually not what you say it is, and if you can change that and look at yourself honestly, it will really change your life.

59

Do you ever wonder what life would be like if you weren't you?

Often. But if I really wasn't me, I wouldn't know it, would I?

60

When you have more kids, will you encourage them to be professional surfers?

I think I'll just encourage my kids to do whatever it is that they love to do. I'm sure when they're two or three, I'll try to put them on a board and hope they love it. But I'd never in a million years get my kids to do something just because it's what I do.

61

Do you want to be married?

Yes.

62

What do you look for in a woman?

Kindness. A friend and I recently had a conversation about the perfect woman, and it centered on a whole bunch of things that have to be natural and that you really can't explain. But the one thing he told me was that there is one quality no one ever talks about in a partner—they have to be nice. I've thought a lot about that since, and I think it might be quality number one. But I'd also always want to be challenged by someone.

63

How would you describe your personality?

Sometimes I feel like a hermit and sometimes I feel quite extroverted. I want to experience life from every aspect, and there are a lot of things I'm only just beginning to learn.

64

What do you consider to be your weaknesses?

Letting myself be pulled in too many ways by too many opportunities, being uprooted all the time.

65

Is there something you really fear?

Getting old and not finding love.

66

What legacy do you hope to leave in professional surfing?

An understanding that surfing is the most fun you can have in life, but it's not life. Life is much bigger than surfing.

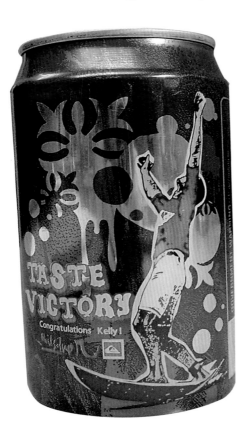

67

What will be the next big challenge for Kelly Slater?

Coming to terms with being off the tour.

68

Is there a wave you keep going back to?

Pipeline, the Superbank.

69

Is there anyone else's lifestyle you'd like to lead for a day?

Yes, I think a homeless person. Maybe somebody with AIDS or who's starving in Africa or who's enslaved somewhere. Maybe someone on their last day of life. I'm thinking the least glamorous lifestyle you could imagine. It's easy to think about experiencing someone's amazing lifestyle on private jets and going to parties, but I don't think I'd learn anything from that.

70

You've had very little self-inflicted negative press. Is that a conscious effort?

Do you mean I've never been caught on one of my drug binges or had a sex tape? Generally people's choices follow them, and I think I've generally made good choices in that respect.

71

Do you find dealing with the media difficult?

Living your life in front of the media can be difficult. It's not easy to have your life scrutinized by people who don't know you.

72

In your case, most scrutiny has come about because of your relationship with glamorous, famous women. Is that part of the attraction?

It's easy to be mesmerized by someone who's got a lot happening in their life, and you're attracted to them. But there is a price to pay when your life is that visible, and it's kind of embarrassing.

73

Are you gun shy? If you fall in love with the most famous woman in the world tomorrow, are you going to run away from it?

I think you've always got to take time to get rid of the negative effects of any situation you've had previously, but if you fall in love, you fall in love. Pretty simple.

74

Are you comfortable with being a role model?

I guess so.

75
Is it hard to be in a good mood for the public all the time?

Yes. I like it to be real, and the reality is you're not always in a good mood.

76
Do you notice people acting differently toward you?

Yes, I do, and when I sense that, I tend to distance myself from that person. I like people to treat me nice like anyone does, but not necessarily different from the way they treat other people.

77
How do most fans act around you?

Good for the most part. Over the top once in a while. Rude occasionally.

78
Do fans ever become friends?

Oh, absolutely. One of my best friends started out as someone who just followed my surfing, and we ended up becoming very close.

79
Is it sometimes hard to stay grounded and humble?

Maybe sometimes. Having people know who you are and having a lot of opportunity is no good reason to forget who you are though. It's actually a good opportunity to set a good example for someone who's gonna remember.

80
What do you do for training?

Bodysurfing. I don't do a lot. I'm actually just entering a period of my life where I'm going to get my body in the best shape I can possibly get it in through diet and training. I'm determined to do that when I'm not on the tour full-time. Other than that, I don't train very much, but I always have wondered how I'd do if I were in my absolute best shape.

81
What makes a good surfer?

Someone who is innovative and does things their own way. Obviously you have to have natural ability and an understanding of how the body connects to the board and how to translate thoughts into lines on a wave. You have to be able to see riding a wave as a performance from beginning to end, and it has to make sense to people who are watching, even if they don't know anything about surfing. Either that, or it's someone who's having fun.

82
What role do you feel you've played in the history of pro surfing?

I was part of a transition in surfing from original thruster surfing to the more advanced surfing. I was lucky to be born at a key time in surfing history, going from twin fins to thrusters and from carving to aerial surfing. I hope I've helped it along.

83
How can the pro tour be made better?

The short answer is, there are too many guys on tour. We need more freedom to run the event during the two- or three-day swell period when the waves are best. Also, if we had a really good wave pool that could make whatever we wanted, where we could control every aspect of the wave at an appointed time with the best surfers in the world riding it, I think surfing would advance way faster, like skating has with vert ramps and parks. Some of the best ideas are right on the fringe, but I think with surfing we have to really take the professional route and not use too many unreasonable choices with regard to competition. People want to see the best of the best. The biggest rivals battling it out in the best surf, head to head.

84
Where will board design go in the future?

I think the main places it's going to go are about strength, repeatability, and waste. We're a dirty industry, and we're starting to get a wake-up call about it. I'm directly responsible for a lot of pollution, using a hundred-plus boards a year. I can't even calculate what that's doing—the fumes, the wasted resin, and where does it all end up? As for board design, I think we'll just trim down a little in size in the near future. There's a little too much board getting in the way still. Self-designing on computers for the average guy isn't out of the question.

85
Do you buy carbon credits?

I do, but there are conflicting reports about whether they work or not. I'm going to buy them whether they work or not because it might be the right thing to do. A study came out recently that said carbon credits don't work except in the case of the trees that got the most water and grew the fastest. That tells me that the trees that grew slower and got less water actually did help in some way. But at the end of the day it's just simple math—the more trees you plant, the

Good
luck
Kelly!

better the air quality. I don't see why you wouldn't just want to be safe about it and do your part. There are so many different views about it. Let's just take the worry out of whether it's true or not and just do the reasonable thing.

86
If you think the advances are going to come in construction techniques rather than design, does that mean the thruster is going to be with us for another thirty years?

I think the four-fin configuration is going to play more prominently in the next few years. Right now it's a fad, but I think they're going to create some traction in the industry. I also think tow boards have helped push general design along really quickly. They showed us in practical terms what had only been theory—that you don't need a big board to ride a big wave, you need a flatter rocker and a straighter outline. You could ride a five-six on the biggest wave you've ever seen if it's designed right. It could have a super-wide tail, too. There are a lot of design elements that are coming from

tow surfing. Boards might get shorter again, and they're definitely going to get stronger, and flex characteristics are going to become more standardized.

Even the average surfer on tour doesn't know a lot about board design. I think all of us need to get more involved in design, to shape more often. A lot of my friends on tour were really quite blasé about their boards. Rob was one who wasn't, but he liked to experiment with single fins and the whole old-school cruising trip. Shane Dorian would get a new board and go, "I don't know much about it, but it's loose and it gets vertical in the pocket!" And I'd be thinking, yeah, but why? What are the fundamental characteristics of design that create that? I think with shaping machines and the other advances, we may be heading for a board that you can actually change. Like you could increase the concave in the bottom, you could thin the rail out a little or take a little flex out. The mutating board will probably happen.

87
How hands-on are you in the shaping bay?

Quite hands on. I'll occasionally take a pass with the planer. I'm generally there, looking over Al Merrick's shoulder. The other day I went in, and we made a board that may not work at all. I called it the Control Freak, and it's based on Cheyne Horan's ideas about control, which were that it came from the curve in the tail. The wider tail allowed you greater control over the maneuverability. It was all about the power being between the feet, which was the opposite of Tom Carroll's surfing, which was about power surfing from the rail, wide point forward. When I went off the tour I tried going in Tom's direction with the

wide point forward, but it just didn't work for me. So we went in and made a basic teardrop shape with wide tail and narrow nose. It's a function creates form shape, which is more or less the way Al and I have worked from day one. We have a really good understanding of each other's ideas, I think.

88
After so many surfboards over the years, is there a board or boards that were really magic?

I've had a number of magic boards. It seems like about every two years or so I'll end up with one. They haven't all been Al's, but more than half have. I've had magic boards from Maurice Cole and Simon Anderson, too. Maurice is a pretty radical designer and more often than not they won't work for me, but when they do, they're really good. Simon's approach is more consistent. He doesn't stray too much from his basic understanding of a good board. It doesn't do everything well, but it carves the face of the wave in the way that Simon does. I think it's awesome that someone as good a surfer as Simon is a great shaper as well. Al is the master of flow and hydrodynamics, of translating a feeling into a board. I can tell him where I want to go on a wave, and he'll make the board to do that.

Photography Credits

Monterey
Bay
Aquarium,
February
2008.